FRIEND IN DEED

WM. PROCTOR SMITH, J.P.
Chairman of the Company
from a portrait by James Gunn, A.R.A.,
on the occasion of the Company's Centenary

FRIEND IN DEED

The History

of a Life Assurance Office

from

1858

as the

REFUGE FRIEND IN DEED LIFE ASSURANCE AND SICK FUND FRIENDLY SOCIETY

to

1958

as the

REFUGE ASSURANCE COMPANY LIMITED
" Refugium Rebus Adversis "

by
CYRIL CLEGG
Fellow of the Institute of Actuaries

Produced and published by Stone and Cox Limited,
44 Fleet Street, London, E.C.4, for the
Refuge Assurance Company Limited, Oxford Street, Manchester.
Printed letterpress by Stone and Cox
using Monotype 'Baskerville' 12 point, 2 point leaded.
Bound by A. W. Bain and Co. Ltd., London, E.2.

To all those who contributed in the past or are contributing in the present so much in a very human and worth-while cause.

Wm Proctor Smith.

Chairman

June, 1958

PREFACE

This is the history of an organisation set up a long time ago by a few men who, ordinary as they might appear to have been from the occupations they followed, yet had the wit to observe a public need, the courage to embark upon meeting it, and the industry to persist through years of stress until the foundations were well and truly laid of a very great life assurance office.

They began by taking life assurance into the homes of people of small means; and though many other aspects of the business are now completely changed, this original principle remains as the basis of that most potent force for national thrift now known as " Home Service Insurance ".

This story of their office, from its initial days as a tiny and struggling friendly society to its present status as an impressive and most successful company, is, in effect, a mirror of the whole history of industrial life assurance as conducted by them and by their friendly co-workers in the industry. It is a very human history, dealing as it does most intimately with the financial aims and ambitions of millions of individuals and hosts of families; and although the original title of the society may have changed, it still remains, as on countless occasions it has proved to be in the past, a true " Friend in Deed ".

The tale is written primarily for Refuge men and women, not only for those presently engaged in all the various forms of the company's activities, but also for that very large number of past employees, now retired on pension, who actually took part in many of the events here recorded. It may not, however, be without interest to a wider circle, whether of past beneficiaries, present policyholders, friends, critics—all, in one way or another, participants in this odyssey.

ix

ACKNOWLEDGMENTS

I am indebted to George Allen and Unwin Ltd. for permission to quote from *A History of Life Assurance*, by Dermot Morrah; to Professor J. F. Rees for the use I made of his book *A Survey of Economic Development*; to Staples Press Ltd. for permission to quote from *An Introduction to the History of Life Assurance*, by Professor A. Fingland Jack; to Dr. Alfred Plummer, for permission to quote from his book *New British Industries in the Twentieth Century*.

The *Manchester Evening News* permitted the use of the photograph shown on page xxii, and *Park Pictures Ltd.* that on page xx. The City Surveyor's Department of the Manchester Town Hall provided me with an old photograph of one of the Company's early premises, reproduced facing page 52.

I must thank also Lt.-Col. G. L. Usher (the Manchester Regiment Association); L. Ashmore (retired General Manager); L. S. S. Bickley (retired Superintendent); H. A. L. Cockerell (Secretary, Chartered Insurance Institute); C. C. Harrison (the Company's Solicitor); R. Jackson (Head of Estates Department); G. F. Maule (Estates Department); S. Murray (Stone & Cox Ltd.); R. F. Pennington (Joint Investment Secretary); H. L. Peterken (Secretary, Industrial Life Offices Association); N. W. Ross (the Company's Actuary); J. Jones (Secretary, Refuge Field Staff Association); E. Woodhouse (Hon. Secretary, Refuge Staff Council).

Most of all, I think, I had resort to W. Brewood (Head of Records Department) who delved so deeply into dusty basements to give me the information I sought; to Alec Taylor (Resident Engineer) whose knowledge of all three buildings proved to be encyclopædic; to Miss M. Cooper (Directors' Secretary) who spent many months examining and making précis of old Minutes extending over many years; and to

Acknowledgments

W. G. Ashton (Head of Publicity Department) whose practical help in the proofing, photography and presentation of this book was quite invaluable.

I am particularly grateful to my colleagues on the Board who not only provided information unobtainable from any other source, but who were an unfailing source of encouragement to

THE AUTHOR

Contents

CHAPTER I

PRE-INDUSTRIAL ASSURANCE   *Page*

Funerary benefits in Roman days: Medieval Gilds: Economic
conditions *circa* 1850: Burial Clubs: Byng's Diary: Need for
organised life assurance   I

CHAPTER II

THE REFUGE MAKES ITS BOW

The " Refuge " is born: Title: Objects: Rules: First Committee of Management and Officers   6

CHAPTER III

EARLY DAYS

Early Struggles: First Office: Absorptions: James Proctor:
Organisation: Agents and Collectors: Remuneration   12

CHAPTER IV

FROM SOCIETY TO COMPANY

Difficulties continue: Re-assurances: Sickness Fund: Henry
Thornton: Robert Moss: Henry Adams: Incorporation as a
Company   20

CHAPTER V

ORGANISATION

New Board of Directors and Officers: Resignation of Wm.
Bradburn: Territorial expansion: Director Areas: The Pim
Hole Club: Annual Report, 1866: Progress in sight   29

CHAPTER VI

DUKINFIELD TO MANCHESTER

Move to Manchester: William Proctor: James Wilcock: Life
Assurance Companies Act, 1870: Statutory Returns:

CONTENTS

Thos. Josh. C. L. Bordman: Valuations: Separation of the
Branches: New Directors: Chief Office moves again   ..   ..

Page

39

CHAPTER VII
RAPID EXPANSION

The Company strides out: First permanent Chairman: Death
of James Proctor: "Transferring": Opening of Number 1
Building, Oxford Street: W. H. Aldcroft, F.I.A.: Death of
Wm. Proctor   55

CHAPTER VIII
LEGISLATION

South African War: Association of Industrial Assurance
Companies and Collecting Friendly Societies: Staff Organisa-
tion: Life Assurance Companies Act, 1909: National Health
Insurance: Death of James Wilcock: First resident Solicitor:
Opening of No. 2 Building   68

CHAPTER IX
WORK AND WAR

Rapid expansion: J. G. Marriott: The First Great War, 1914–18   84

CHAPTER X
REORGANISATION

Reconstruction: Blocking of Debits: General Inspectors:
General Insurance: Formation of Staff Associations: Pension
Scheme: Industrial Assurance Act, 1923   91

CHAPTER XI
BETWEEN THE WARS

Post-War Depression: Death of R. W. Green: War Memorial:
Diamond Jubilee: Death of Philip Smith: The General Strike:
House Purchase business: Manchester Civic Week: Death of
Jas. S. Proctor: Allocation of profits to industrial branch policy-
holders: New appointments at Chief Office: World-wide
financial crises: Expense ratios and valuation bases: Cohen

CONTENTS

Inquiry: Opening of No. 3 Building: Superannuation Trust *Page*
Fund: Transfer of Eire business 102

CHAPTER XII
1939—1945
The Second Great War, 1939–1945: Administrative difficulties:
Civilians under fire: Bomb damage: Death of J. Proctor Green 116

CHAPTER XIII
INDUSTRIAL ASSURANCE AND POLITICS
Beveridge Report: National Insurance Act, 1946: Industrial
Assurance and Friendly Societies Act, 1948: Anti-national-
isation campaign: Industrial Assurance Council 124

CHAPTER XIV
MODERN DEVELOPMENTS
Modern ways: Grant of Arms: First President: War Memorial
Plaque: Letting of No. 3 Building: Entry into General
Insurance: London Investment Office: Quotation on Stock
Exchange: Mechanisation: Publicity: Reconstruction of
Capital 128

CHAPTER XV
THE PIONEERS 136

ENVOI 142

APPENDICES
The present Board: Office-bearers, past and present: Comparative statistics 143

⬤⬤⬤

HOW THE COMPANY CELEBRATED

⬤⬤⬤

Illustrations

The Chairman:
Wm. Proctor Smith, J.P. .. .. Frontispiece

Facing page

James Proctor 4
George Robins 5
Hart Street, Manchester, as it is to-day 12
Astley Street, Dukinfield 13
Certificate of Insurance 20
Opening pages of Treasurer's Book 21
The Fifth Annual Report 28
Early Policy 29
Wm. Proctor 36
James Wilcock, J.P. 37
Henry Thornton, J.P. 44
Henry Adams 45
11/13 Corporation Street, Manchester 52
85/89 Corporation Street, Manchester 53
Agreement with the Liverpool Victoria Legal Friendly
  Society 60
No. 1 Building, Oxford Street, Manchester 61
Philip Smith 68
Jas. S. Proctor 69
John Harrison 76
The Tower, No. 2 Building 77
R. W. Green, J.P. 84
Volunteers from Chief Office, August, 1914 85
W. H. Aldcroft, F.I.A. 92
General Inspectors, 1919 93

ILLUSTRATIONS

Facing page

War Memorial 100
Diamond Jubilee, Free Trade Hall, Manchester 101
Robert Moss, J.P. 108
No. 3 Building, rear view and private roadway 109
Notice to evacuated Policyholders 116
Bomb damage: Southampton Office, Before and After .. 117
J. Proctor Green, J.P. 124
J. Wilcock Holgate 125
War Memorial Plaque 132
Grant of Arms 133
The Present Board 140

CHAPTER I

Pre-Industrial Assurance

FUNERARY BENEFITS IN ROMAN DAYS: MEDIEVAL GILDS:
ECONOMIC CONDITIONS CIRCA 1850: BURIAL CLUBS: BYNG'S
DIARY: NEED FOR ORGANISED LIFE ASSURANCE.

INDUSTRIAL assurance, which is fundamentally the provision of funds
for the funeral expenses of a deceased member, is by no means a modern
concept.   From very early days men have desired to offset, in so far as
lay in their power, the financial strain on their households to which
their deaths would give rise.   Long ago, the Romans had organisations known as " collegia " which functioned in very much the same
fashion as the burial clubs of the early industrial era and for precisely
the same reason.   These collegia, though organised for a variety of
mutual purposes, bore a common distinguishing mark in the religious
element which pervaded them in greater or lesser degree; but in time
this element became weaker and other aims came to the fore,
prominent among them being the provision of a fitting burial for the
members.   Professor Fingland Jack in his introduction to the *History
of Life Assurance* refers to one such collegium dated A.D. 136.   The
rules provided for the payment by new members of an entry fee in cash
together with " an amphora of good wine ": thereafter each member
paid a small monthly contribution of 5 *asses* (about 2½d.)   The total
contributions formed a pool to provide the payment of a lump sum on
the death of a member, out of which was allocated a proportion
amongst those other members attending the funeral, who were, of
course, put to some expense to come. There is an analogy with present-
day methods in that to prevent fraud the collegium could only pay the
money to the testamentary heir.   If no such existed, the expenses of the

I

burial were paid by the collegium itself, no other interest being recognised. There were regulations relieving the society from liability in cases where the monthly subscription was a certain amount in arrears; and in cases of suicide all claims were forfeited.

After the passing of the Roman Empire and the collegia, there still remained the urgent need felt by men to provide for themselves a fitting burial. For centuries this appears to have been met by the formation of associations of men living in the same area, or in the same village, or engaged in the same occupation, with this object in mind. In time these led to the establishment of the trade or craft " gilds " which became very prominent in medieval times, concerned in many activities, but always including that of supporting the responsibilities of the head of the family towards each of its members. Thus the gild chest was open to those whose circumstances compelled them to borrow money, thereby preserving them from pauperdom and maintaining their self-respect. Permanent distress was dealt with by the grant of a stipend. In times of sickness grants were made during the period of incapacity; and an honourable burial was provided for a poor brother.

A man would take no shame in claiming help from his gild. In a sense it was his family, which he and his like had organised for their mutual protection, and his affairs would be dealt with in a personal and understanding way. It was very different when, partly through political action, and partly through the widening of the boundaries of industry, the gilds disappeared, as indeed they did, with the notable exception of the twelve livery companies of London, which still exist to-day. All that was left was the operation of the Poor Laws of Tudor days and, for many years, these continued alone as the last resort of the distressed.

The industrial revolution, though now regarded as a product of the nineteenth century, had in fact been gradually proceeding from a much earlier date. It was by no means, however, the initiation of plenty for all. The general rise in the standard of living was to come later—much later: and in the early days, although the wealth of the country grew increasingly rapidly, that of the individual, generally speaking, did not. A man remained faced with the hazards of sickness or death with little to spare from his earnings to make provision against them. It was the day of the " parish ", the " workhouse ", the " union ", the " pauper's grave ", and against any one of these indignities the soul of the individual revolted. With the sturdy spirit of independence which distinguished the people of that time, men took steps in their own defence by the formation of friendly societies, sickness or burial or trade clubs—the last being a type of gild and the forerunners of trade unions.

An interesting reference to the operations of these societies appears in the diary of the Hon. John Byng, in 1792, in which this passage occurs:

"At Macclesfield I put up at the best tho' a bad Inn (where I have been before), The Angel, where the House was so crowded by a grand dinner that I betook myself into a small Room behind the Bar, desiring to be served from the Remains of the grand Dinner; 'And pray, of whom is the Club formed?' 'Why of old women of this town who having established a fund for the benefit of their helpless, their Sick, etc., and for funerals, meet at this Inn to settle their accounts, and to Enjoy themselves over a good dinner' from part of which, particularly a good Ham, I dined. (Their subscriptions, not missed at the payment, are a most excellent Invention, strengthening the bands of Fellowship, destroying the chains of Poverty, and rendering overseers of the Poor needless) ".

A contemporary traveller, François de la Rochefoucauld, *circa* 1784, describes with enthusiasm the universality of the village sick club, with its annual dinner to pass the accounts. For, he observed, " the English always conduct their business around a dinner table; it is thus they are happiest and most liberal ".

Looking back, one can perceive in that closing sentence a warning of what might—and indeed of what often did—come to happen. A village community, closely knit and self-contained, was one thing; the floating groupings of working people, created so extensively by the industrial revolution, were quite another. Burial clubs and the like

3

were still needed, and continued to be widely created—but without the natural cohesion and traditions of their village predecessors, and only too often, as it unfortunately happened, without their standards of probity. There is no doubt that there were abuses of what was basically a praiseworthy aim. This was, perhaps, a natural consequence of the manner in which the local sickness and funeral clubs operated, the method commonly adopted being to make a levy on the members whenever a death occurred, coupled in some cases with the payment of small weekly contributions at a flat rate. This very " hit or miss " system very often failed to function satisfactorily, a contributory factor no doubt being that the headquarters of the club were nearly always at a public house, the only club the industrial workers possessed. All too often it was the funds that were buried rather then the members.

Once again history was repeating itself. The Roman collegia also appear to have adopted a flat rate of contribution and not to have made any differentiation between old and young entrants, or between good and bad lives. In their case, too, there was always the possibility of a compulsory winding up through lack of funds. Professor Jack refers to an interesting inscription discovered in one of the wildest parts of what is now Rumania dealing with such a case. It recites *inter alia* that the president had not made an appearance at the college since his election; that the treasurer had rendered his accounts to the members present; that there was no more money in the chest to pay funeral expenses; that the society possessed no more burial places; and finally says " For a long time no one has wished to meet on the days fixed by the laws of the collegium or to pay the dues. The foregoing is made known to all so that if one of the members comes to die he shall not imagine that the collegium still exists and that he has the right to make any claim ". That was written in A.D. 167; but about the middle of the last century prior to the development of modern industrial assurance the words would have had quite a familar ring.

JAMES PROCTOR

GEORGE ROBINS

Pre-Industrial Assurance

Dr. Alfred Plummer in his *Survey of the development and structure of new British Industries in the Twentieth Century* says that one of the most important functions of inventors and industrialists is to study the general features of the trend of demand and adds

" The normal sequence is, firstly, the realisation or belief that there is a latent or potential demand for a certain commodity or service; secondly the invention and perfection of appropriate productive methods based upon research and the consequent growth of knowledge; thirdly, the marketing of the new commodity or service."

There is no doubt whatever that the demand for some such service as was rendered by sick and burial clubs was very real. The cold and impersonal operation of the Poor Law was no solution—indeed it was so hated as to promote the formation of clubs even though these often failed adequately to meet the need. Clearly something better was required, something more firmly established and more reliable. Not only was this appreciated by certain far-seeing men, but also there were conceived certain basic ideas by which the demand could be met—or in Dr. Plummer's words " produced "—by such means as the spreading of the risk by covering larger areas and a greater diversity of people; by appropriate rates of contribution; and by regular collections in the homes of the members. Finally it was realised that it could only be marketed by actual selling by full-time representatives. There still exist to-day clubs of the ancient sort, but they remain local, small, and do no more than originally they set out to do. The organisations built up on the principles enumerated above include the great industrial assurance offices of the present time.

CHAPTER II

The Refuge Makes its Bow

So far as the Refuge is concerned it all began in 1858—one hundred
years ago.   What caused a handful of individuals to meet together to
discuss the formation of a new society, it is hard to tell.   They seem to
have been men of quite ordinary stature, whether socially, industrially
or intellectually.   There was little prospect of gain, but the certainty
of work and worry.   They were venturing on the ground of existing
local clubs, which would render them a cordial dislike and a determined
opposition.   Yet clearly their new type of society was needed and they
set out boldly on their course.

It would appear that preliminary talks began early in 1858, and
were continued for some months before that most significant decision
was taken to found " The Refuge Friend in Deed Life Assurance and
Sick Fund Friendly Society ".   What a pity it is that the first minute
book has vanished, and with it any record of the meetings and discussions which took place before the final step was taken!   Good
fortune, however, has preserved for us the original cash book, in which
the first entries are dated October 21st, 1858, two months before the
Registrar certified his approval of the rules.   These entries record the
payments for 2s. 6d. shares in the embryo society issued to men who
subsequently became its first officers, and from others who took part in
the building of it.   It may well be asked how it came about that a
friendly society issued shares.   The reason is " wropt in mystery ".
It can only be surmised that it was done in fact to get some working
capital, and that this fashion of getting it was due to—as Dr. Johnson

said once as regards a mis-spelling in his own dictionary—" pure ignorance ". It was one of the several oddities of the early days, which should be appreciated whenever further reference is made herein to these society " shares ".

The original rules were most beautifully set out in 17 pages of copperplate, at a cost, as recorded in the treasurer's book, of £1 5s. They begin by stating the objects of the society:

" To raise from time to time by regular and special subscriptions from the several Members thereof a stock or fund for any of the following purposes, viz:

Firstly, for insuring a sum of money not exceeding £200 to be paid on the death of a Member to the Widower or Widow of a Member as the case may be or to the child or relatives of such Member for defraying the expense of the Burial of a Member or of the Husband, Wife or Child of a Member.   Secondly, for the Endowment of the Members or nominees of Members."

In addition, a sick fund department was created, of which males and females between the ages of 10 and 55 could become members, and under which a weekly sum would be paid in the event of incapacitation through sickness or accident, together with free medical attendance and medicine, or the sum of 1s. 6d. per week in lieu.

They conclude with the following certificate from the Registrar of Friendly Societies:

" I hereby certify that the foregoing Rules of the Refuge Friend in Deed Life Assurance and Sick Fund Friendly Society at 15 Hart Street Manchester in the County of Lancaster are in conformity with law and that the Society is duly established from the present date and is subject to the provisions and entitled to the privileges of the Acts relating to Friendly Societies.   The Rates of Contributing and payments are not stated to have been prepared by any Actuary.

JOHN TIDD PRATT

The Registrar of Friendly Societies in England.
December 20th, 1858

I hereby certify that the foregoing 17 pages contain a copy of the Rules of the " *Refuge friend in deed Society* " which are deposited in my office.

(Signed) JOHN TIDD PRATT
August 2nd, 1859

So the society was duly established on a basis which contained within itself both good and bad. The good was that which required " regular " subscriptions, whereby the society recognised the weakness of the *ad hoc* contributions which had been so often, and so naturally, the downfall of many of the sick and burial clubs. Within the society contributions were by age in accordance with the rates set out in the schedule annexed to the rules, or as later might be determined. The weakness was indicated by the words in the certificate which pointed out that the rates of contribution and payment were not stated to have been prepared by any actuary. It is extremely unlikely that they *had* been; experience was soon to suggest that further consideration should be given to this vital factor in the society's operations, and within a few years the rules were amended.

Who was it who first gathered a few friends about him and made the suggestion that a new friendly society be formed ? What manner of men were they with whom he conferred ? Precise answers to these questions are not to be had, but there is strong circumstantial evidence to throw light on the beginning.

The original officers and committee of management were as follows:

Trustees:

THOMAS WARD	..	Astley Street, Dukinfield
JOHN JONES ..	..	Chapel Lane, Wigan
THOMAS FLETCHER	..	New Town Pemberton

Treasurer:

JOE ROBINS ..	..	Broadbottom

Committee of Management:

THOMAS WARD	..	Astley Street, Dukinfield
JOHN HASELDEN	..	126 Chapel Lane, Wigan
JOE ROBINS ..	..	Broadbottom

WILLIAM BRADBURN	..	Dukinfield
THOMAS SINCLAIR	..	St. Andrew's Terrace, Newtown, Wigan
JAMES PROCTOR	..	Preston
JAMES WOODCOCK	..	Oldham
GEORGE ROBINS	..	15 Hart Street, Manchester
JOSEPH SMITH	..	Stockport

Secretary:
GEORGE ROBINS   ..

Auditors:

JOSHUA FRANCE	..	Lord Street, Oldham
JOHN SLACK ..	..	Oldham

As has been said, there is no precise record of who was the enterprising individual to whose mind there was presented the brave idea of entering the troubled sea of sickness and funeral assurance. Generations of Refuge men have thought it was James Proctor, always referred to as " The Founder ". He may well have been so, although he was never chairman, nor did he immediately take the leading part in the management of the new venture. Alone of the founders, however, his name has been continuously and actively associated with the Refuge from that far-off day a hundred years ago, and it seems not unfair to continue to attribute to him his honorific title.

William Bradburn appears to have been a man of great enthusiasm, with a dynamic personality which impressed itself upon his colleagues. Although the society did not have a permanent chairman, someone being elected to that office at each meeting, Bradburn appears to have been so appointed almost continuously until 1866, and he played a prominent part in advancing the interests of the new venture. What his occupation—if any—formerly was, we are not sure: which is a pity, since a man of such enterprise must surely have had within him the possibilities of success in a variety of fields, and it would be interesting to know whether, and in what connection, he had previously used the talents he undoubtedly possessed.

Two other men closely connected with Bradburn were the brothers Robins—Joe and George. There is a typical touch of the north in the affectionate diminutive "Joe" rather than the formal Joseph. Joe was the infant society's first treasurer, and continued so until his death in 1862. His account books are in the simplest form, merely a record of cash received and cash paid, and they were beautifully kept. They show how often he advanced money to keep things going; and the committee quite certainly owed much to his work, and financial assistance. It is small wonder that on his death the members resolved that " We, the committee cause to be placed at the Head or foot of the Grave of the late Joe Robins a memorial of the respect that we bear to him ".

His brother George was the original Secretary. What his occupation was we do not know: but it is on record that he became a grocer and corn dealer, and continued in that capacity throughout the remainder of his connection with the Refuge, which lasted until his death at some date about 1870. He also followed the pleasing practice of his brother in advancing money to the society, without interest; until one day the committee appear to have been seized with compunction, and resolved " that George Robins be allowed the sum of Twelve Shillings and Sixpence for Interest for monies advanced, and that he be allowed to charge the Society Interest or loss that he may be at through advancing money to the Society ".

Of the remaining members of the original committee, two only take their place in this history as playing important parts in its unrolling. They are James Woodcock and James Proctor. The former was a tailor and draper, and it was from Oldham that he came to further the work of the society. His value does not appear to have depended on his powers of salesmanship so much as on his administrative ability—

which was presumably considerable as he remained in office until his death in 1884, and up to a year or two before this date was commonly elected to the chair at committee meetings and annual gatherings. In a Return to Parliament dated August, 1867, his name is entered under the heading " President "—though probably only because the space was there and seemed to require to be filled !

James Proctor was a man of a very different sort, naturally perhaps as his occupation was given as that of " general agent ", which suggests the work of a travelling salesman. In addition, he practised as a journeyman tailor; and such a man, possessing such abilities, was just what the Society needed. Proctor appears to have seen the necessity for a widening of the area of operation, and a greater diversity in the type and occupations of new members. In his travels he had the opportunity to carry out these requirements, and well indeed he seized it.

These were the outstanding men amongst the founders. Of their colleagues, nothing very much is recorded, and one by one they disappear from the scene, whether through lack of confidence in the venture, lack of interest, lack of ability, we do not know. It must be admitted that in the early years the shareholders must have needed an unusual degree of courage and vision to persist in what appeared for so long to be a hopeless cause.

CHAPTER III

Early Days

EARLY STRUGGLES: FIRST OFFICE: ABSORPTIONS: JAMES
PROCTOR: ORGANISATION: AGENTS AND COLLECTORS:
REMUNERATION.

THE first conversations of the founders must have taken place in the
summer of 1858, if not before, for by the autumn of the year the project
was well beyond the talking point. As has already been said the
initial financing of the scheme was by the issue of 2s. 6d. shares.
Heading the list of subscribers was Thomas Ward, who was to become
a trustee and who contributed £1 5s. for ten shares on October 21st,
1858. With others on the same day and subsequently to January 5th,
1859, there was put up between them the sum of £22 12s. 6d.
Among these subscribers were William Bradburn and James Proctor
who each took ten shares on November 5th, 1858. Further subscriptions were to come in during the months that followed: and
desperately were they needed in those early years when so often we find
the society owing money to the treasurer to keep itself going.

This was in no way surprising, and indeed was the common
experience of other similar institutions which took their rise about that
time. This new type of society was different from its predecessors, the
" clubs ". The novel idea had to be introduced to prospective
members, opposition from competitors had to be overcome, a collecting
staff had to be built up and provision made for its remuneration—
indeed, the wonder is not that the financial path was so difficult, but
rather that it was eventually found possible to survive.

There are some revealing entries in the Cash Books:

12

Hart Street, Manchester, as it is to-day

Astley Street, Dukinfield

1859.	May 6th.	Ann Higham, advanced the sum of £3 to be paid in 14 days.			
	August 8th.	Cash advanced by Joe Robins:	£15	9	4½
	October	— ditto —	2	2	1½
	December	— ditto —	3	10	3
1860.	May 4th	Geo. Robins, wages in part ..	2	13	3
		Paid by Committee of Management to balance		2	0
1862.	Sept 23rd.	Loan from George Robins ..	25	0	0
1863.	April 11th.	Balance in hand	1	0	1½

The principal—and at the outset the only—office of the society is shown in the Registrar's certificate attached to the rules as being at 15 Hart Street, Manchester. This was probably purely a matter of convenience, it being the home of George Robins, the newly appointed secretary: and in the summer of the following year the office was removed to 59 Astley Street, in the little Cheshire village of Dukinfield, about six miles from Manchester, where William Bradburn resided. The modest rent is recorded as being £3 per quarter. The reasons for the move are not very clear, a possible explanation being that Dukinfield adjoined a busy industrial area, and that it was probably thought advantageous for the infant society to cut its teeth in an area in which the forceful Bradburn was well known.

The distinction of being the first agent to pay in premiums to the treasurer belongs to a member of the committee, John Haselden, who had the further, though perhaps doubtful, distinction of presenting for payment the first three death claims in February and March, 1859, for £9 0s. 2d., £1 13s. 10d., and £2 respectively.

As illustrating the knife-edge along which the young society was making its way, it is to be noted that by June, 1859, it was the sum of these claims which represented practically the whole amount by which outgoings to date exceeded the income. Following the payment of those claims it is intriguing to read an entry: " John Haselden to save a death, 2s. 4d." What, one is inclined to wonder, lies behind that brief note?

A considerable fillip was given to the finances of the society through the agency of William Bradburn who, on the Refuge behalf, took shares in two loan clubs, the Quiet Gill Money Society and the Crescent Inn Money Society, both of Broadbottom, from which were borrowed respectively the sums of £49 in August, 1860, and £32 10s. in July, 1861. The following year another of the society's representatives gave evidence of enterprise beyond that required by the run-of-the-mill activities of a collector by persuading the committee to take over the engagements of the " (Late) Working Man's Benefit Society, Macclesfield " including the whole of the funds amounting to £18 1s. Obviously the liabilities came over with the assets, but it is pretty certain that they were accepted with complete equanimity, the important thing at that time being to increase the society's income. This was the first taking-over of the business of another society by the Refuge, and it must be regarded as a tribute to the reputation and prospects of the latter, judged by the rather elementary standards of the times.

As if to emphasise the benevolent aspects of the society's operations —and doubtless because it was entering the field of friendly society work—it had begun life as the Refuge Friend in Deed Life Assurance and Sick Fund Friendly Society: a wordy title indeed. So evidently the founders came to think, and possibly the policyholders also, for in September, 1860, it was resolved that the name be changed to " The Refuge Life and Sick Friendly Society ". Thereafter the society went under this name on some documents, and under the title of the Refuge Friendly Society on others. This last name appears on the earliest certificate of insurance which has survived the years.

It was issued on December 22nd, 1862, on an infant named Henry Pratt, then aged one year, and living, presumably with his parents, in Thistle Street, Manchester. The sum assured was £3 at a premium of one half-penny per week. The benefit was a constant sum and did not increase gradually to an ultimate sum at age 10, as became the custom in later years, when the child had survived what were then the lethal years preceding that age. The certificate bears no mention of a policy: but others dating from a year or two later indicate that on the strength of the certificate a policy might be had on application to the chief office on payment of 6d.

Young Pratt's certificate was issued almost exactly four years after the society commenced business. It bears the progressive number 16075—evidence of the industry with which the agents and collectors were carrying out their task and of the readiness of the public to take advantage of the facilities offered for their protection.

In the constant search for new entrants into the society, the Refuge took a further step in 1863 by taking over the Manchester and Salford Independent Burial Society as a going concern. The proceedings are recorded as follows:

June 9th, 1863

At the Manchester Arms Corporation Street Manchester a Meeting was held for the purpose of arranging with the Committee (appointed by the Members) of the Manchester and Salford Independent Burial Society for transferring the Members of that Society to the Refuge.

*　　　*　　　*　　　*

" Resolved that the Manchester and Salford Independent Burial Society do join the Refuge Life and Sick Friendly Society held at Astley Street, Dukinfield."

*　　　*　　　*　　　*

" Resolved that we the Committee and Trustees of the Refuge Life and Sick Friendly Society do accept of the Members of the Manchester and Salford Burial Society ".

*　　　*　　　*　　　*

Resolve that we advertize.

*　　　*　　　*　　　*

" Resolved that the Manchester and Salford Burial Society has been amalgamated with the Refuge Life and Sick Friendly Society."

Moved by JOSEPH SUTCLIFFE.

Seconded by WILLIAM WINFREY.

(*Signed*) WILLIAM BRADBURN, *Chairman.*

Two days later at a special committee meeting the following resolution was passed:

" That we advertise the following in the *Manchester Examiner and Times*: To the members of the Manchester and Salford Burial Society: This is to give notice that all members of the above-named Society who are desirous of joining the Refuge Society will please to leave their addresses with the district agent, 45 Livesey Street, Manchester."

The district agent here referred to is James Proctor, who had now removed from Preston to Manchester. He was still described as a general agent, but it is a fair assumption that his insurance activities were growing rapidly. Clearly he found it more convenient to be in the principal city of industrial Lancashire, both for the work of the society and for convenience in getting to and from Dukinfield. Probably this far-seeing man already felt that the offices of the organisation would eventually return to Manchester, and wisely, he wanted to be on the spot. It is interesting to record that the Refuge had an office in Livesey Street for over 40 years, and that even when it was moved to a neighbouring main road the title was retained—presumably on sentimental grounds—for another 50 years until at last it was changed to correspond with the then situation of the district office.

The organisation of the society was of the simplest kind. The treasurer, for example, kept a book in which were recorded on the one hand cash received, and on the other cash paid out. According to the rules, a monthly balance was made, and in May of every year, at the general meeting of the members, a report, signed by five members of the committee and the secretary, showing the position of the society was read to the members together with the auditors' report and the balance sheet. As regards the actual operation of the society, it must be remembered that at the outset, and indeed for some years to come, there was nobody serving the organisation full-time. Basically, there were agents in charge of areas—themselves part-time, who appointed and supervised local collectors, also on a part-time basis. One old document dated December 31st, 1866, lists the occupation of some of the latter:

Name	Residence	Occupation	Emoluments for Year ending 31.12.61		
			£	s.	d.
WM. KENYON	Preston	Hand Loom Weaver	1	11	3
CHAS. MORTON	Dukinfield	Collector of Debts			
JOHN ROBINSON	Allithwaite	Stone Mason	6	0	2
JOSHUA COOPER	Broadbottom	Block Printer	1	10	7½
JOSEPH WYCH	Heaton Norris	Weaver	2	17	6
ALFRED ASHWORTH	High St., M/C.	Tin Plate Maker	2	4	0
JOHN ROWBOTTOM	Chisworth	Band Maker	1	6	8
DAVID HURST	Wigan	Mechanic	1	0	2
SELINA LEADER	Staveley	Agent	15	12	0

The last name causes a surprise. A woman agent one hundred years ago seems hardly within the accepted course of events; yet Selina Leader, as a collector, not only existed—as later did many of her sex during the two Great Wars—but, like them, probably proved herself extremely efficient at the task which for some reason she was called upon to carry out.

The original character of the Refuge is clearly indicated in the occupations of the collectors named above. None of them were in clerical jobs and thereby in restricted circles. The society was operated for the benefit of the industrial classes, and its collectors were chosen therefrom as being persons likely to have a wide circle of friends or acquaintances who might welcome the benefits the Refuge could provide. There is no precise scale of remuneration to be discovered in the old records, and terms of appointment varied from case to case. Some men had a small—a very small—salary to encourage them at the start of their insurance careers. Others had " bonus "—up to 12 weeks' premiums—with perhaps a salary later to mark their success. All, it seems, had a commission on their collections, usually, but not always, of the order of 12½ per cent.

As regards the officials at the head office, it would appear that the secretary and treasurer were each paid a salary of £1 per week—and at first, often enough, probably considered themselves singularly lucky to get it. In 1862, Wm. Bradburn was voted 12s. a week for his services, and in the following month was advanced to 30s. a week. George Robins, the secretary was also granted an increase making his salary £1 8s. a week. Each member of the committee was to receive £1 for attending each committee meeting. In a spirit of optimism in March, 1863, the committee gave themselves 10s. a week as salary— but they very quickly repented and two months later resolved that " the committee do not receive any Weekly Salary until the society has in hand the sum of £200 Clear, and not then so as to reduce the sum under £200." With finances as they were to continue for a long time to come, that appears to have been the end of the weekly salary.

At the same meeting it was resolved that the secretary, George Robins, who had moved out from his Hart Street home in Manchester " be allowed half the costs of a half-yearly Contract Ticket between Mottram and Dukinfield." Since the distance is only five miles the full fare for a full year could only have been very small; but every penny counted in those days, which explains the rather careful grant of " a half of a half" to a most valuable servant—a grant, incidentally, which does not appear to have been renewed at the end of the half-year.

With so modest a standard of remuneration it is small wonder that employment with the society was on a spare-time basis. But better days were to come, though not until the committee had managed to weather several more years of crisis and concern.

CHAPTER IV

From Society to Company

DIFFICULTIES CONTINUE: RE-ASSURANCES: SICKNESS FUND:
HENRY THORNTON: ROBERT MOSS: HENRY ADAMS:
INCORPORATION AS A COMPANY.

THE difficulties referred to in the preceding chapter were not caused by
any failure to obtain new business. Policies were numbered as issued
in consecutive order and the records tell of contracts being issued by
the thousand. Thus one policy issued in December, 1862, was
numbered 16,075; another in May, 1863, 23,431; yet another in
November, 1864, 63,851. For so young an office, new business of this
magnitude can only be considered most promising: what was much
more difficult was to keep the expenses within manageable limits.

In any concern, even in these modern days, the costs of expansion
must always be a strain on finance, which is properly met out of
reserves: but in the early days of industrial life assurance, the only
reserves were to be found in the capital initially subscribed by the
shareholders, and this could easily be absorbed by even a slightly
unfortunate claim experience in the early days. Under the original
rules, policies could be issued for sums assured up to £200, and no
doubt proposals were accepted for amounts within this range, claims
under which could not have been met out of the scanty resources of the
society. There are entries, however, in the minutes which indicate
that the committee were alive to the risk, and they took steps to cover it
by means of re-assurance. In at least one case the re-assuring office
was the *European*, for a sum assured of £200—a choice which might

The Refuge Friendly Society,

WITH WHICH IS AMALGAMATED

The Working Man's Benefit Society.

ESTABLISHED, 1858.

Empowered and Enrolled pursuant to the Act 18 and 19 Vict., chap. 63.

CERTIFIED BY JOHN TIDD PRATT, Esq.

CHIEF OFFICE:

ASTLEY-STREET, DUKINFIELD, NEAR MANCHESTER.

This is to Certify, that the following persons have been admitted Members of the Refuge Friendly Society, and have duly made the Declaration required by the Rules of the said Society.

Progressive Number.	Name.	Residence.	Age.	Weekly Premium.	Date of Entrance.	Sum at Death. £ s.
1675	Henry Pratt	4 Thistle St. Oldham Road Manchester	1		Dec 15th 62	3 .

CONDITIONS.

From three months to seventy years, free to half benefit in *13* weeks, full benefit in *26* weeks.

This Certificate shall become void if the members shall die under any of the following circumstances :—

Being on the high seas (except in passing from one part of the United Kingdom to another, or on board of a decked vessel within the limits of Europe in time of peace), unless license shall have been obtained from the Committee of Management, and such additional premium paid as they shall require.

By Suicide or Duelling, within the space of three years from the date of entry.

By Prize-Fighting, or Justifiable Homicide.

A member can, at any time, by writing, nominate his or her widower, or widow, or children, or any particular child, as the person or persons to receive the amount specified at his or her death.

When the sum exceeds £50, and the member neglects to nominate, the amount specified will be paid to his or her Executors or Administrators.

When the sum does not exceed £50, and the members of the Committee of Management are satisfied that no Will was left by a deceased member, and that no Letters of Administration will be taken out to his or her effects, the sum specified will be paid to the widower, or widow, or children, or the next of kin of the deceased member, as shall appear to the Committee of Management to be entitled to receive the same, without taking out Letters of Administration in England or Ireland, and without Confirmation in Scotland.

Any members having any disease upon them, and not making the same known to the officers of the said society at their entrance, will not be entitled to any benefit. Any member being six weeks in arrears will not be entitled to any benefit.

Certificate of Insurance

Opening pages of Treasurer's Book

well have been unfortunate in view of the failure of that office some years later.

In the numbering of policies, no distinction was made as between the various types offered to the public, whether sickness, endowment or burial insurance. The committee kept a careful eye on the experience of each of these classes and it would appear that they were not too happy as regards the sickness branch. Too large a proportion of the new business came under this head, and it is very certain that it was never a paying proposition. Poverty and malnutrition amongst industrial workers were rife, and claims upon the sick fund were frequent. Another adverse influence lay in the scanty means of communication of those days, and it was impossible to set up a comprehensive system of sick visitation, without which no proper check could be maintained over sickness claims. It is no matter for wonder that the committee soon became uneasily conscious that they had, as it were, a bull by the tail. They did do something about it, however, for although in the revised rules issued in February, 1863, the scheme was retained, it was made subject to the new condition that no person should be admitted a member of the sick branch, nor remain such unless he or she was also a member of the burial branch. In addition, medical examination was required in all cases, and not only " if required " as set out in the original rules. Despite these very reasonable steps, it appears to have been decided later that it would be better to close the branch altogether to new entrants, and it was accordingly resolved in May, 1863:

" That no person be admitted a member in the Sick Department after May 31st (1863) and that it be optional with the secretary and chairman whether any be received during that time from any districts."

Quite what was meant by this resolution is a matter of some doubt, for sickness contracts continued to be issued. Once again, however, in 1866, the matter came up for consideration, and at a meeting on January 8th, a resolution was passed as follows:

"That the Sick Branch be done away with: that six months' notice be given to the agents".

It needed some courage to come to such a decision: but resolution was lacking as regards sticking to it—understandably perhaps, for the society badly needed premium income and the original friendly society did more business in the sick branch than in the burial section.

This position really arose out of the fact that of the two evils ever facing the poorer classes, sickness or death, it was insurance against the former which was more often chosen, it being better to live, when sick, out of the hands of the " parish " even if that disgrace had to be suffered after death.

The business was, no doubt, originally included in the objects because the rules of the society were drawn up on the usual friendly society lines. The main business of an industrial assurance office is, however, burial and endowment assurance, which should certainly not be a local affair, but which should involve the acceptance of proposals from any part of the country in which agents or collectors can be found to operate: and with the widening spread of the society's activities it became increasingly difficult adequately to supervise the sickness branch. The committee did the best they could and by maintaining a policy of continuous discouragement managed to put a stop to the issue of new policies by 1872, the existing business being allowed to run off as a closed fund. As is the common experience of such funds, many years were to elapse before the last policy disappeared from the books: and in fact the sick fund did not disappear until as late as 1944, with the death of the last surviving policyholder—who had been in continuous membership for 78 years, and one way or another had done remarkably well out of it.

Throughout its existence, the business maintained its quality of non-profitability as may be seen from the following figures:

Sickness Fund

Period	Premiums received	Expenses	Claims Paid
1865–76	£3,533	£1,095	£2,428
1901–19	524	19	1,617
1920–38	146	2	904
1939–44	8	—	23

It was indeed well that the committee were strong enough to impose their will, despite its unpopularity amongst the business-getters, and thus to avoid the risk that brought so many other organisations to failure, i.e., for the sake of present income to continue a business which it was impossible financially to support.

About this time steps were also taken to tighten up the organisation, and to secure increased efficiency of administration at the centre. A special meeting of the members called in March, 1863, was notable for its election of a new committee of management. The original committee had consisted of nine members including the secretary and treasurer. The number was now reduced to six:

*WM. BRADBURN, Astley Street, Dukinfield, Cheshire.

*JAMES PROCTOR, 45 Livesey Street, Manchester. General agent and journeyman tailor.

*JAMES WOODCOCK, Fletcher Street, Oldham, Lancashire. Tailor and draper.

J. H. FERRAND, High Street, Glossop, Derbyshire. Oil and tallow agent.

*GEORGE ROBINS (Secretary), Broadbottom Bridge, Mottram, Derbyshire. Grocer and corn dealer.

GEORGE BRIDGE (Treasurer), 53 Kershaw Street, Bury, Lancashire. Commission agent.

* Original member

George Bridge had taken the place of the late Joe Robins: at half his salary, i.e., 10s. a week. All six were still spare-time workers: and three of them already had the advantage of being travelling salesmen in their own lines of business.

With a smaller committee composed of men who were not only strong personalities, but who were also taking a prominent part in the recruitment of new members, the collection of premiums, and the paying of claims, there was a quickening of the society's activities which was to lead, eighteen months later, to its conversion into an office incorporated under the Joint Stock Companies Act, 1862. It was resolved that there be appointed a lawyer for the society—a wise step having regard to the legal difficulties into which the new society, in its new and unexplored field of activity, could not but fall. The choice fell upon a Mr. Darnton, a name frequently to be noted in the minutes for the coming years. It was resolved also that the rent be paid every week; it is interesting to speculate as to the moving force in this very sensible business provision—was it landlord or tenant?

The years 1862 and 1863 were something of a vintage period as regards recruits to the staff. Three men were appointed whose names have now become part of Refuge history. One of them joined the office staff: the other two were field men who worked throughout in the areas to which they were first appointed and which they were eventually to control. One of these latter was Henry Thornton, whose name first appears in the treasurer's book on July 28th, 1862, as having sent in his first collection, i.e., 3d. From this modest beginning he made rapid progress, and after six months he was returning sums in excess of £1: excellent figures by the standards of those early days. His area was Warrington, from which he never moved. He became a director in 1872, and remained on the board until shortly before his death in 1920.

In August, 1862, the rapid influx of new business rendered it necessary to consider the provision of extra help in the head office, and Wm. Bradburn and George Robins were empowered " to appoint a fit and qualified person " as and when the need became apparent. An assistant was in fact appointed in October of that year: whose influence for decades was to be as great as that of any other of the pioneers. He was Robert Moss, destined in time to be the secretary of the Refuge and a director. He was to give loyal and devoted service for a period of 61 years before his eventual retirement, a length of time which has only been exceeded by one other individual, S. G. Leigh, F.I.A., formerly general manager, and at present still a director.

Robert Moss came into the office as general factotum, serving both the secretary and the treasurer as occasion demanded, attending to the wants of members of the public who called, and to the collectors and agents who came in to pay in or draw out. The treasurer's cash book in its later pages bears entries in his beautiful copper-plate. The minutes of a number of committee meetings are in his hand, though not all, as if George Robins had turned over his notes to Moss to copy into the minute book as necessary. In later years, when Moss was more firmly established, minutes and various notes on meetings are inscribed in this handsome calligraphy which is a delight to the eye and reflects no doubt the more leisurely tempo of business life in those days as compared with the rush and bustle of to-day.

It seems typical of the doubtful regularity of salary payments by the struggling society that the first mention of Robert Moss is to be found in an entry in the treasurer's cash book dated November 29th, 1862, " Paid Robert Moss eight weeks' wages, £8." There is evidence of his confidence in the concern in an entry in the " cash received " side dated December 1st, 1862: " Robert Moss £5 " presumably a subscription for shares.

Another name of significance appears in a resolution dated June 11th, 1863:

" That Henry Adams of 208 Fitzwilliam Street, Sheffield, be allowed the sum of five shillings per week for an Office Rent and that the office be at his house at the aforesaid place, and that he be also allowed full 12 Weeks' Bonus ".

In Refuge history the name Adams is always associated with Sheffield, for it was into that area that Henry Adams first introduced the society and subsequently for many years was in control of its operations there. He became a director in the same year, 1872, as Henry Thornton, and remained on the board until his death in 1906.

Before we leave the very interesting year of 1863, it should be recorded that the first step was taken along the long road of mechanisation, in a resolution dated October 7th of that year:

" That a copying press be bought the first opportunity, to be a good one and cheap ".

Here again there is to be observed evidence of the committee's careful watch over expenses, and their typically north country determination to get value for money: to be confirmed four months later in another resolution passed upon an application from one of the agents for office equipment:

" That if Lentton wants an office desk he must buy one at his own Expense."

There is no doubt whatever that the difference between a society which began operations and failed, and another which survived, lay almost entirely in the ability or otherwise to control the heavy expenses which were the inevitable concomitant of expansion. The main charge was the remuneration of the agents and collectors, which was made up of two elements—bonus, which represented a procuration fee of a certain number of weeks' premiums in respect of each new policy issued, commonly twelve: together with a running charge for maintained collection of premiums at varying rates, but mostly of the order of $12\frac{1}{2}$ per cent. Each new case, therefore, was at once a financial strain on the office; whilst in addition, of course, there were the accompanying charges in respect of rents, postages, travelling, salaries, etc. In the absence of the most frugal oversight there was every risk of an inability to build up the necessary reserves to cover the steadily increasing liabilities. So frequently did this happen in fact, and societies become unable to continue, that the matter developed into one of such public interest as to come under the notice of Parliament;

and although the evils were naturally exaggerated—it has always been the case that sin is news, whilst virtue is not—the whole business of assurance, whether ordinary or industrial, was put under examination by Mr. Gladstone, in 1864. His solution was to set up a Government concern under the Postmaster-General to conduct life assurance in competition with the existing offices—but without that one essential feature of industrial assurance, the collection of premiums by visiting agents. It is no part of this history to recount how, if only by reason of that significant lack, the scheme was a complete failure: but the possibility of such a competitor was sufficient to induce the committee of the Refuge to consider how best they might meet the new circumstances. Their decision was to disassociate themselves from the friendly society movement altogether, and to turn their office into a limited company.

The actual resolution put forward at a special meeting of members on September 1st, 1864, reads perhaps amusingly, but is certainly expressed with clarity and decision:

" That this Special General Meeting of the Members of the Refuge Life and Sick Friendly Society duly convened, hereby express its thanks to the Committee for the Honourable way in which they have conducted its affairs up to the present time, and finding that it is the Intention of the Government to still interfere with the Government of Friendly Societies, with the view of bringing them under Government officials to find place and pension for the needy sons of the Aristocracy: Be it therefore resolved that the business of the Refuge Life and Sick Friendly Society be and is forthwith incorporate with the Refuge Friendly Society Limited and that the committee do take immediate Steps to carry this resolution into effect forthwith on the passing of this resolution."

A special meeting of the board of directors of the new organisation then took place. It had one short resolution before it, which was adopted unanimously:

" That we receive the whole of the Business and funds of the Refuge Friendly Society and that all liabilities accruing from the said Society be paid by the Refuge Friendly Society Limited ".

(*Signed*) WILLIAM BRADBURN
Chairman

So passed the old Refuge Friend in Deed. There were still to be anxious years ahead, but the change-over was to inaugurate a new era of stability for policyholders, staff and the company itself.

THE FIFTH ANNUAL REPORT

OF

THE REFUGE
Life & Sick Friendly Society,
HEAD OFFICE: ASTLEY-STREET, DUKINFIELD.

ENROLLED BY ACT OF PARLIAMENT.

RESPECTED MEMBERS:

In presenting you with this report, the committee have great pleasure in announcing that they have again extended the society's business in various parts of the empire, where its benefits had been previously unknown, but is now being hailed with pleasure, by those for whom it was specially designed to benefit. Owing to the almost unparalleled depression in the cotton trade, affecting most vitally the interests of the working classes, the arrears of the members are unusally large.

During the period over which this report extends (nine months,) the reason of this being a nine months account is, the committee desiring to have the books properly examined by the auditors, and finding that the returns only reached the secretary's hands at the latter end of April, did not give time, on account of the extraordinary rapid increase of business to the society. Your committee have received 18,149 proposals for new members during the nine months; this is a proof that the Refuge Society is approved of by the working classes, for whose benefit it was especially designed.

It is again our pleasing duty to return thanks to the gentlemen composing our medical staff, for the assiduity and skill they have displayed in attending to the members who have come under their care. Our thanks are also due to the agents and collectors generally, for the care and pains they have taken in selecting lives; and the committee hope for again having their hearty co-operation, and that they will not slacken in their effort in this direction, as so much of the society's welfare depends on their prudence.

Your committee would press upon all members, as well as agents and collectors, the desirability of increased exertion in the coming year. Let each one feel that it is a duty incumbent on him to spread a knowledge of the society far and wide. No similar society has made, or is making such rapid progress.

In conclusion, your committee have every confidence that the accompanying Balance Sheet will meet your approbation; and we hope still to show more favourable results in our next report.

We remain, yours, the Committee,

WILLIAM BRADBURN, *Chairman,*
GEORGE BRIDGE,
JAMES PROCTOR,

JOSEPH HENRY FERRAND,
JAMES WOODCOCK,
GEORGE ROBINS, *Secretary.*

Statement of Accounts, from March 31st, to December 31st, 1863.

DR.	£	s.	d.	CR.	£	s.	d.
To Balance from last report	973	17	0½	By Death Claims	1212	15	6
— Contribution, Burial Branch	2615	15	2	— Sickness Claims	110	1	6
— Ditto Sick Branch	251	11	9½	— Endowments	266	16	9
— Ditto Endowment Branch	368	7	0	— Medical Fees	18	17	2½
— Sale of rules and Cards	33	16	10½	— Commission	483	1	9½
— Interest	24	13	6	— Printing and Stationery	68	3	7
— Rent	3	2	0	— Office Fixtures	15	16	0
— Old Furniture	0	10	0	— Rent and Taxes	17	2	0
— From Hanley County Court on ac. of S. Lightfoot	0	10	0	— Advertisements	11	3	0
				— Gas and Coals	2	3	3
				— Postage and Parcels to agents	30	0	8
				— Ditto ditto from agents	28	18	2
				— Salary to President	67	15	0
				— Ditto Secretary	56	0	0
				— Assistants	60	0	0
				— Auditing account	2	5	0
				— North Stafford Infirmary	0	10	0
				— Balance in favour of Society	1880	13	11¾
	£4272	3	4¾		£4272	3	4¾

MANAGEMENT FUND.

DR.	£	s.	d.	CR.	£	s.	d.
To Balance from last report	74	17	2½	By Travelling Expenses in Opening Districts	39	7	0½
— Contributions	433	6	4	— Committees' Salary and Expenses	80	0	0
				— Salaries to Agents and Rent	110	13	0
				— Balance	278	3	6
	£508	3	6½		£508	3	6½

GENERAL STATEMENT.

	£	s.	d.
To Balance brought down	1880	13	11¾
— Ditto Management Fund	278	3	6
— Office Fixtures	37	14	0
— Books on hand	120	0	0
	£2316	11	5¾

RESPECTED MEMBERS:

We, the undersigned, have received from the secretary the statement of accounts of this society, (for the past 9 months only, ending Christmas 1863,) together with the whole of the books, and other documents belonging thereto, and we have great pleasure in announcing to you that we have found them *strictly correct.* And we are sure that great praise is due to the secretary, for the straightforward manner in which he has kept the accounts of the society.—It is with great pleasure we draw your attention to the increase of the society, being 80 per cent on last year, which fact speaks highly of the untiring energy, with which the business of the society has been conducted during the past nine months, taking into consideration the times, and the competition of other societies. The progress of the society is owing to the combined exertions of the committee, together with the chairman Mr. Bradburn, and secretary Mr. Robins, and agents, and they being determined to gain the highest position, will in the end succeed.

ROBERT MOSS,
CHARLES MORTON. } Auditors.

H. Burgess, General Printer and Bookbinder, 40 Wharf-street, Dukinfield.

Fifth Annual Report

The Refuge Friendly Society,

WITH WHICH IS AMALGAMATED

The Working Man's Benefit Society.

ESTABLISHED, 1858.

Empowered and Enrolled pursuant to the Act 18 and 19 Vict., chap. 63.

CERTIFIED BY JOHN TIDD PRATT, Esq.

CHIEF OFFICE:

ASTLEY-STREET, DUKINFIELD, NEAR MANCHESTER.

Fortnightly

No. 18721-243 Premium £ 0 - 0 - 9½   WEEKLY Sum Assured £ 0 - 8 - 0 *one* 8 - 0 - 0 *for Husband*
IN SICKNESS.   *at death* 6 - 0 - 0 " *Wife*

Whereas, *Edwin Worril*
West Melton. Wath

the person hereby Assured, hath proposed to become a member of the **Refuge Friendly Society,** by affecting an Assurance with the said Society, to endure during the whole continuance of h *is* Life, for a specified benefit in case of Sickness, or incapacity from labour, arising from bodily accident, being *Thirty-two* years of age next birthday, and having duly made the declaration required by the Rules of the said Society.

Now this Witnesseth, That in consideration of the payment of the sum of *Nine pence half penny* this day made to the Society, the receipt whereof his hereby acknowledged, and also in consideration of the future payments of the like sum to be made at the office of the said Society, on each and every subsequent *Fortnight* to the date hereof in this and every succeeding year during the Life of the said Assured, the Funds and other Property of the said Society shall, and they are hereby declared to be subject and liable, upon proof from our Medical Officer of the sickness of the said *Edwin Worril* to pay to h *im* the weekly sum of *eight Shillings* during the continuance of that and any future sickness.

And it is hereby Declared, that the said Assurance is effected under, and in pursuance of the Rules of the said Society, and the same is and shall be subject and liable to the several conditions, restrictions, and stipulations therein contained, so far as the same may be applicable thereto, and to the conditions hereupon endorsed.

Given under our Hands, this *Sixteenth* day of *February* One Thousand Eight Hundred and Sixty *Three*

Entered *R M*   *William Bradburn* CHAIRMAN.
Examined *GR*   *George Robins* SECRETARY.

Early Policy

CHAPTER V

Organisation

IT was at the annual meeting of the members of the Refuge Life and Sick Friendly Society on May 2nd, 1864, that " it was suggested also that it would be better if the Society was Registered under the Joint Stock Companies Act, 1862. It was then moved and seconded that the Board take steps for that purpose and get Articles, etc., ready as soon as possible ".

The committee, however, had anticipated the decision of the annual meeting, and as early as February 3rd had held a meeting specifically to consider the possibilities. It was moved and seconded " that we form a Joint Stock Friendly Society and that it be called ' The Refuge Friendly Society Limited ' if legal, if not legal then to be called the Refuge Society Limited ". The capital was to be £25,000, with power to increase, divided into 5,000 shares of £5 each. A later meeting in March rescinded the £5 share resolution and decided in favour of 12,500 shares of £2 each—a denomination which remained unaltered until the re-organisation of the company's share capital nearly one hundred years later. Two shillings and sixpence was to be paid on application and a similar sum on allotment. Each director was to take up 25 shares and to pay one shilling per quarter per share. The qualifying holding for directors was to be 25 shares—a holding which similarly remained unaltered for nearly a hundred years. At a

29

later meeting in July it was resolved to make calls at five shillings per share every three months. It was also resolved:

"That we invest our money in the Bank of England or the Manchester and Liverpool District Banking Co."

There is no record of any recourse being had to the Bank of England: but the company's present bankers are the District Bank Limited, a development of the Manchester and Liverpool District Banking Company, and so are old friends of 94 years' standing.

Naturally enough, the members of the committee resolved that they should form the board of the new company. At a later meeting they appointed Wm. Bradburn as the manager, with George Robins as secretary, and George Bridge the treasurer: Bradburn, Bridge and James Proctor to be the trustees.

The annual meeting in December, 1865, accepted the suggested composition of the board, but did not agree that Wm. Bradburn should be the general manager. In his stead they appointed George Bridge to this position, George Robins remaining as secretary. No mention is made in the minutes as to the appointment of a treasurer or trustees and quite possibly no such appointments were made. They belong more properly to the friendly society world from which the Refuge was emerging; and indeed, at a meeting in 1884, a proposal, strongly supported, that the company should have a treasurer was turned down.

The directors' fees were fixed at one guinea per week: and it was realistic indeed to agree in September, 1866, that at the next meeting " each of the Board to receive 10s. 6d. on a/c of Board wages and the other 10s. 6d. to go towards paying their Shares up ".

Although the Refuge Friendly Society Limited had taken the place of the Refuge Life and Sick Friendly Society, taking over the whole of its engagements both to policyholders and to staff, it is very curious to observe how obstinately the latter refused to die. Indeed, it would appear to have carried on an existence concurrently with that of the

new company for several years, for at a board meeting in June, 1866—
two years after the transfer of engagements—it was resolved that

" a deputation of 3 go to London to see Mr. Tidd Pratt as to the Best way of
bringing the Business of the aforesaid Society to a close ".

As a matter of fact there is nothing in the records to show that the
business ever *was* brought to a close: and as late as January 1st, 1867, a
return was made to the Registrar by The Refuge Life and Sick
Friendly Society for the year 1866 in which the total contributions
were shown as:

Burial branch ..	..	..	£56 19s. 1½d.
Sick ,, ..	..	..	£104 0s. 2½d.

It is difficult to avoid the thought that the persistence of the old
society, in some fashion or another, was due not only to the possible
reluctance of members to accept the new company in place of the
society to which they were accustomed—which probably involved a
collector in acting for the same organisation under different names!—
but also to differences of opinion on the board. Certainly in 1866,
Wm. Bradburn fell foul of his colleagues: for a special meeting of
directors was called for September 21st of that year to take into consideration the " trouble and disrespect " that Bradburn had brought
on the society. To quote the minutes: " after talking matters over
pro and con, Mr. Bradburn gave in his resignation ".

He was clearly not without his supporters, for there is contained
within the minute book a cutting from some unknown newspaper
which reads: " Will the late Chairman of the Refuge Friendly Society,
Correspond with the Committee now formed for preventing Dissolution of said Society—Address O.Y. Post office, Sheffield (in
confidence)".

Nothing appears to have come of this advertisement, for Bradburn
was never employed again by the society, nor was the dissolution
affected in any way other than by delay. It was an unfortunate ending

to an association which had brought great benefit to the original venture. Bradburn was clearly a forceful personality, and probably not the easiest of colleagues with whom to work; but then the same could be said of his fellow members of the board, as is evident from the bluntness of their discussions and decisions even as regards one another as recorded in the minutes. Perhaps the solution of the mystery is to be found in a resolution of the board that Bradburn be allowed a gratuity " for the purpose of obtaining medical and other assistance (he being now out of health)".

It has been remarked that an industrial assurance office cannot remain a local organisation. Its life blood is premium income, which can only be secured—and what is more important, maintained—by casting a wide net. This the Refuge did: and from their centre in and around Manchester—for that was whence came the bulk of their early business—the committee began at once to explore other areas. Evidence of this is contained in the early minute books where collectors are mentioned for what they have done—or sometimes for what they have *not* done—in the districts in which they were working. Thus we read of Joseph Roper, of Hyde, in June, 1862; of James Marshall (who was " to be allowed 4s. per week to canvass members in the Barnsley district "); Charles Hackley, at Fenton (who alas! had absconded and taken away the books and the property of the society); Edwin Eastburn, who was engaged as agent for Sheffield, and allowed the expenses of removal and 5s. per week as salary. And there was policy-holder, Henry Wiggans of Newcastle, who whilst on sick pay broke the rule forbidding absence from home between sunset and sunrise and " was excluded from the society for being out after hours." So the story unfolds, and within the period 1862 to 1864 we find men operating in or appointed to Wigan, Wakefield, Huddersfield, Ulverston, Runcorn, Hebden Bridge, Hull, Todmorden, Hanley, Warrington, Leeds (" *Ellis should do more business*", *said the committee*), Eckington, Oldham, Worksop, Staveley, Chesterfield, Bradford, Halifax, Macclesfield,

Congleton, Wilmslow, Alderley, Chorley, Knutsford, Birmingham, Stockport, Nottingham, Derby, Dudley.

The Refuge was an " industrial " concern, and it took itself to where industry was, and where their potential policyholders resided. The above list is as it appears chronologically at various meetings of the committee of management, and it is interesting to observe the fashion in which from its home town of Dukinfield in Cheshire it extended its operations further into Cheshire, and into the adjacent counties of Lancashire, Yorkshire and Derbyshire. There is evidence of a thrust down into the thriving Midlands: and clearly this policy of expansion was to continue. Naturally enough, in those days of difficult communications, it followed the railways: it is a true saying that development follows communications. Eventually, the society was to arrive in London, and the rules issued in 1872 bear on the cover the following statement:

Chief Offices:
Corporation Street, Manchester,
and
78 Myddleton Street, London, E.C.

A beginning with a system of regions or districts had been made at a special meeting of the committee in August, 1864. It was then resolved that

" Wm. Bradburn be appointed agent or Superintendent for Yorkshire and all Districts under Sheffield District: and that Proctor takes Lancashire ".

The remaining districts would be in Cheshire, and presumably could be administered from the head office at nearby Dukinfield. An enclave in Proctor's region, consisting of Bury, Bolton and Burnley, was allotted to George Bridge on distinctly curious terms. The fact was that Bridge from time to time had tided the society over difficult financial periods by the loan of monies, and the sums owing to him after nearly four years' operations were considerable. To meet the situation, the committee, at a special meeting on the day following that

33

on which the agreements with Bradburn and Proctor were made, made an agency agreement with Bridge which virtually turned him into a one-man office.   The minute of August 23rd, 1864, reads:

" Moved and seconded that George Bridge be allowed the following Districts, viz., Bury, Bolton and Burnley for a term of Fourteen Years, and that he pay all Claims for Death and Sickness in the said Districts and the Surplus in the Burial and Sick branches shall go to liquidate the debt owing to him and at the end of Fourteen years he shall give up all Claim on the aforesaid Districts.   But all Monies Collected in the Endowment, Annuities, Accidental and Fire Branches or any other Branches except (life and sick) shall be sent to the office less Commission and he shall pay for all Cards and all Claims made on the Society in the aforesaid Branches (except life and sick) shall be paid from the office.   In the event of the aforesaid George Bridge dying before the said Term of Fourteen Years the same shall be carried out for the Benefit of his Heirs, Administrators or Assignees ".

In the light of the later appreciation of the mathematical basis underlying sick and burial assurance the assumption in the above resolution that the difference between premiums collected and claims paid constituted disposable monies was shortly to be realised for the fallacy that it is.   At the time, however, it was not uncommonly held; with the result that only those offices survived which could collect sufficient sums in premiums to cover not only claims and expenses but also to enable funds to be set up to cover the increasing liabilities.   It is a chastening thought that even to-day there are folk who hold that it is unnecessary to build up such funds.

George Bridge's office-within-an-office was known for years as the " Pim Hole Club ", the name being taken from the area in Bury in which he resided.   The name is amusing but the underlying idea is understandable: even to-day Refuge policyholders often regard themselves as members of " Mr. so-and-so's Club ", Mr. so-and-so being the office representative who calls on them so regularly, and whom they know so well.   In the case of Bridge, the title " Pim Hole Club Collector " was actually printed under " George Bridge " on the contribution cards issued to policyholders in his area.

One way or another, 1866 was to prove a trying year for the company. It was, of course, short of money: the continued rather vague existence of the old " Friend in Deed " organisation must have been a disturbing influence: the looming difficulty regarding Mr. Bradburn probably had its effect on progress: and plans for a move to Manchester were under consideration. To cope with the financial difficulty it was resolved on January 8th:

" that we receive Money on Deposit and Issue Debenture Bonds and the Interest be 6 per cent. for one year, 6½ per cent. for two years and 7 per cent. for three years and upwards ".

Whether this venture—which seems from our modern standpoint to have been distinctly dangerous—had any appreciable success is not known, but there must have been some response since we have a resolution on February 16th, 1866

" That J. H. Ferrand and James Woodcock work the Loan Branch jointly (and in their absence the Secretary attend to it) and the salary allowed to Ferrand previous be divided equally between them."

There was an attempt to strengthen this part of the office's activities a little later in the year by the taking-over of a loan and discount company which was separately owned by the directors of the Refuge. This concern was a small affair which did not do a great deal of business, and it does not seem that the Refuge had a great deal of success in this field. On the other hand, it must have attracted some amount of money to the new company, which was still very much in the position where every little helped.

A large part of the financial strain was caused by a rapid influx of new business, in itself, of course, a most desirable feature: and success in this field really meant that the society, although delicately poised, was on the verge of leaving its early troubles behind and setting out on a career of solid progress. That certainly seems to have been the view of the directors in their report to the shareholders on July 12th, 1866:

" Your directors have the pleasing duty of congratulating you on the satisfactory

35

progress of the society, which has not only been equal to the expressed anticipations, but has far exceeded them for, in addition to the old Business which is far in excess of that done in the previous Year, the new business has proven of the most profitable Nature. The new kind of assurance transacted by the Society since the change has moreover had the effect of recommending the Society to the Notice of an entirely new class of assurers whose good opinion and high position have increased the facilities of your Directors for extending the operation of the Society among the Industrial Sections of the community. From the formation of the Company to December last (i.e., a period of sixteen months) 28,963 Policies have been Issued while no less than 374 proposals were declined or not accepted at the additional rates charged. These two facts prove that while the favor with which the transactions of the Society have been viewed has materially increased, your Directors give more attention to the permanent stability of the Society than to the more immediate extension of its operations.

" During the period under review we have lost 1,182 members by death in the Industrial Department. In the Sick Department of the Society the claims have continued to increase in a more rapid ratio than your Directors anticipated. Your Directors trust that by the more effectual supervision now exercised these slight Causes of Dissatisfaction will speedily disappear.

" In conclusion, your Directors would tender their best thanks to the whole of Medical Staff for the careful and efficient manner in which they have Performed their various duties.

" To their Legal Advisers for the care, attention and interest they have shown in their Department and also to the whole body of the Agents for their attention to the future interests of the Society and feel assured that while the Directors and other officers continue thus to work in Perfect harmony our Past Success great as it has been may be regarded as only the Harbinger of our future Success and future Magnitude."

(Signed) GEORGE ROBINS, Secretary.
JAMES PROCTOR.

In view of the position of affairs at that time, the report can hardly have been as pleasant to the directors to write as it was for the share-holders to read. Yet though the hopes it contains may have been stressed in somewhat too optimistic terms, nevertheless there were four remarks in it which were genuinely encouraging. In the first place, to issue 28,963 policies in sixteen months was true expansion: and there is no reason to doubt that the company in its new form really was entering

Wm. Proctor

JAMES WILCOCK, J.P.

a field in which were to be found better types of life as prospects for assurance. Once again the unfortunate sickness fund comes up for mention: once again it is stated that the business is unsatisfactory and that efforts are being made to improve it. Apparently the wisest step would have been to implement the resolution of the previous January: " That the sick branch be done away with " and another in the following May: " That agents must not push the sick business at all ". In practice the abolition of new sick business was a gradual process, and as has already been said was only completed in 1872.

The kernel of the report is the statement that " your directors give more attention to the permanent stability of the society than to the more immediate extension of its operations ". This was probably quite true. There were too many examples around them of concerns which had *not* followed this principle; and the directors of the Refuge were far too sensible and hard-headed not to take warning from them.

The hope that " the directors . . . continue to work in perfect harmony " is rather ironical in view of the impending resignation of Wm. Bradburn. Subsequently his place was not filled and affairs continued in the hands of the remaining five. It would be unfair to say baldly that from now on the affairs of the society were to prosper; the fact is that the tide was at last to turn for the company, and would have done so even had Bradburn remained. The bleak circumstance of an empty till, with income just about balancing expenditure, was gradually to recede, and funds and reserves were to start out on their long and difficult road of accumulation.

It is at this stage that the directors in charge of areas were to prove their worth. They were now James Proctor (Lancashire), George Bridge (Bury, Bolton and Burnley), James Woodcock (Cheshire, Liverpool and Sheffield). All three worked together to manage Yorkshire, the area left vacant by Wm Bradburn. Their work involved constant vigilance, continuous travelling, staff appointments, settlement of disputes, fixing of terms of remuneration, even the drawing up of new scales of sick benefit—indeed, in the light of modern practice they seem to have functioned in some ways as travelling head offices. Certainly they had wide powers, and their ability to take decisions on the spot was most valuable to the young and now rapidly expanding company.

Although George Bridge continued in the position of general manager, affairs at head office seem to have been left to the secretary, George Robins, and his assistant, Robert Moss. The latter was clearly making his value apparent in this capacity, for in October, 1866, we have a blunt resolution: " That we don't employ Mr. Moss as agent for Bradford." His was clearly to be an inside career.

The guiding principle for the directors was very clearly stated in a resolution in April 13th, 1866:

" That in the opinion of this Board the present financial position of this Society renders it at once desirable that steps should be taken to make the Income meet the Expenditure ".

After eight years of experience the harsh facts had made themselves evident. They were met: and they were overcome.

CHAPTER VI

Dukinfield to Manchester

MOVE TO MANCHESTER: WILLIAM PROCTOR: JAMES WILCOCK: LIFE ASSURANCE COMPANIES ACT, 1870: STATUTORY RETURNS: THOS. JOSH. C. L. BORDMAN: VALUATIONS: SEPARATION OF THE BRANCHES: NEW DIRECTORS: CHIEF OFFICE MOVES AGAIN.

IT has already been mentioned that a project was under consideration to move the head office to Manchester. Evidently the accommodation in Astley Street, Dukinfield, which after all was only one of a terrace of dwelling houses, was quite insufficient for the growing company; whilst moreover, a more central and accessible situation was becoming a necessity. Accordingly, in December, 1865, it was resolved

" that we take an office in Manchester and that Mr. Woodcock and Mr. Proctor see after a suitable one ".

This they did with commendable promptitude and on January 8th, 1866, it was resolved.

" that we take the office in Albert Street, Manchester, on the best Conditions for 7 years and that James Woodcock, James Proctor and J. H. Ferrand go and see the landlord ".

That however was the last to be heard of Albert Street.

Next there is talk of a move to Blackfriars and at a meeting in July, 1866, the board resolve quite definitely

" that we take an office in Manchester for the Head Office and that we take the one situated in Blackfriars."

Once again, with a not unusual but most aggravating absence of any reason, nothing comes of this resolution either; it is not even rescinded; simply a new one is passed in August,

" that we take the office in Corporation Street, No. 13 ",

39

and so at last they did, at a rent of £30 per annum. They were soon to find out however, that they had underestimated the rate of growth of their office: and in April, 1874, the adjoining premises, numbered 11, were added, excepting one room then occupied as a barber's shop, on a five years' lease of the two, at a total annual rent of £70. Here the company was to remain for another four and a half years.

It is interesting to observe how persistently throughout the minutes the theme of economy recurs. The lessons of the year 1866 had been well learned, and every expense appears to have been carefully scrutinised—and if not justifiable in the eyes of the board the unfortunate person who incurred it had to stand it himself.

In June, 1867, two typical resolutions are passed:

" that in case an agent of this society . . . get himself into trouble with any other Society and contrary to Instructions, he shall bear all Expenses incurred "
and

" that this Society do not go to any Law Expenses in any ordinary cases that if any agent or collector gets contaminated in Law Expenses without the Knowledge of the Board, they shall pay their own expense ".

The past participle employed may not have commended itself to the legal profession, but its warning could hardly be mistaken.

But it was not only the staff to whom discipline was applied. The members of the board were just as forthright and demanding towards one another. Not one of them appears to have been at all hesitant to criticise a colleague. Any departure from instructions was visited with rebuke and often a fine; and the meetings had to be properly conducted. An interesting resolution dated July, 1868, reads:

" that the Board receive 10s. 6d. per week on a/c. of Board Wages the first to be paid on Friday Week, and any member of the Board not being in the office 15 minutes within the time stated he shall forfeit 5s. for the Week providing any of the Board be absent through Sickness he shall forfeit according to the decision of the Board should any Director be off on the Society's Business he shall not be fined at all but he must give Notice of going away any Director coming in a state of Intoxication he shall not be allowed to sit on the Board for that day and shall forfeit his wages for the week ".

Autre temps, autre moeurs!

About this time the need appears to have been felt for the appointment of some officials who could advise the board on matters of finance. The original society had appointed J. H. Ferrand, James Proctor and George Bridge as a finance committee; and now the new society was to follow its example. It was accordingly resolved in March, 1868, " that there be a Finance Committee of Two Members of this Board besides the Secretary " and " that George Bridge and James Proctor form the Finance Committee along with the Secretary ". It was a sensible and, as events were to turn out, a far-seeing move, for although at the moment there were no funds to invest, the time was soon to come when investment of moneys would become a very important part of the work of the company. For the time being the thing was to keep the Refuge ship on an even keel; and at least two members of the committee had experience of what that meant, as both Bridge and Robins had from time to time lent the office appreciable sums to tide it over emergencies.

There used to be a story current in chief office of a clerk whose father had been connected with the committee some long time previously and who used from time to time to exhibit a very large gold watch descended in the family, saying impressively that many a claim had been paid in the old days on the strength of that valuable security. The story may be apocryphal—many stories in chief offices are. But it deserves to be true, for certainly on occasion it must have been hard to know where to turn for funds to keep the business going.

In the same year it was decided to fill the vacancy on the board left by Wm. Bradburn; and on May 18th, 1868, it was resolved

" that William Proctor be appointed a Director of this Society, and that he receive not any wages until £300 be paid for shares".

An odd sort of resolution, the underlying reason not being apparent.

As a consequence, as was no doubt intended, the new director did not attend any board meetings for some considerable time. Whether he took part in the general meetings is not on record; he was undoubtedly working with his father, James, in the field, in Lancashire. He was eventually to become chairman and general manager.

This year, 1868, is to be remembered for another reason—the appointment to the staff of James Wilcock. It appears that his father had held an agency with the Refuge since its earliest days but had taken comparatively little interest in it. His son James, however, had other ideas, and after completing his apprenticeship gave more and more of his time to the agency, until in 1868, at the age of 22 he was appointed district manager for Blackburn, and henceforward devoted his whole energy to the society's business. His first office was on his father's premises in King Street, Blackburn; and it is amusing to relate his grandiloquent title of "district manager" to his total staff—two spare-time agents. He was later to become a director and subsequently chairman, a position he held until his death in 1912.

In 1870 there occurred an event which was to affect profoundly the life assurance companies of this country, whether ordinary or industrial. For a number of years the governing authorities had been greatly disturbed by scandals arising out of the insolvency of a number of life assurance offices, culminating in the classic failures of the " Albert " and the " European ". It was the age of the early development of life assurance, and all too often it was carried out on faulty lines. Charles Dickens in *Martin Chuzzlewit*, writing of an imaginary company, the " Anglo-Bengalee Disinterested Loan and Life Assurance ", describes the secretary as a man who " fully proves to you that any connexion on your part with that establishment must result in a perpetual Christmas Box and constantly increasing Bonus to yourself, and that nobody can run any risk by the transaction except the office, which, in its great liberality, is pretty sure to lose ". Dickens also quotes the chairman of this fictitious company as saying to a friend: " ' Whenever they [the policies] should chance to fall in heavily, as you very justly observe they may, one of these days; then ' he finished the sentence in so low a whisper, that only one disconnected word was audible, and that imperfectly. But it sounded like ' Bolt ' ' ".

The natural result of the existence and demise of these unsatisfactory concerns was to invoke legislation; and on August 9th, 1870, there was passed " The Life Assurance Companies Act, 1870 " which was to mark an epoch in the history of British life assurance, and profoundly to affect the future of the offices.

First and foremost the Act placed life assurance on the mathematical basis which truly underlies it. The calculation of premiums is a scientific affair and it is not enough merely to receive premiums, account for the claims and expenses, and regard the remainder as profit. This is a fact which at the time was not completely comprehended, if indeed at all. The proper professional adviser was an actuary, duly qualified by examination; but in 1870 there were few such qualified specialists about. It was a new and little known profession; and indeed although the term "Actuary" was used in the Act, it was not defined. As a result, the duty laid upon the actuary periodically to make an investigation into the financial condition of a life assurance company was carried out on occasion by persons of rather vague qualifications. Nevertheless the Act established the principle of scientific valuations, and before the end of the century the unqualified man was very much the exception.

The requirement of the preparation of a revenue account and balance sheet in statutory form for submission to so august a body as the Board of Trade must have given the directors, with their rather elementary ideas of book-keeping, food for some thought; and they came to the conclusion that it would be well to obtain professional assistance. As an actuary was certainly going to be needed for the financial investigation due under the Act in five years' time, it was very sensibly decided to find some person who could fulfil the dual duty; and the choice fell upon a Mr. Bordman, LL.D: an almost legendary figure, known affectionately to generations of actuarial students at chief office as " Thos. Josh ", from the form of his signature which commonly took the form " Thos. Josh. C. L. Bordman ".

It is possible that he may have been associated with the company earlier as a lawyer, for it was he, in great part, who conducted negotiations with John Tidd Pratt, the Registrar for Friendly Societies, over the winding up of the " Friend in Deed ". He was in fact a solicitor, the senior partner in Bordman and Co. of Southwark, London; a doctor of laws; and later a fellow of the Statistical Society. He was presumably a mathematician of parts, and took to himself the title of " actuary " as had others contemporary with him. He was never, however, qualified under the examinations of the Institute or Faculty of Actuaries.

His first duty, no doubt, was to explain the meaning of the Act as a whole and to advise the directors as to their future legal obligations. His next was to assist in the preparation of the first accounts to be rendered in respect of each of the years 1870 and 1871, and—rather gratuitously perhaps—to prepare an actuary's report to the board in respect of the latter year. This report is, however, a valuable piece of history, including as it does some significant figures regarding aspects of the business not covered by the accounts, expressed in rather optimistic terms, and including what looks like a little special pleading. It reads as follows:

ACTUARY'S REPORT

To: The Directors of the Refuge Friendly Society Limited.

Gentlemen,

I have carefully perused the Papers submitted to me and I am of opinion that the Refuge Friendly Society Limited is in a sound and prosperous condition.

The number of new Policies issued during the past year being 12,372 is of itself a proof that the Society is well adapted to meet the numerous requirements of the

HENRY THORNTON, J.P.

HENRY ADAMS

working classes in respect to life assurance and that its objects and benefits to them especially are well understood.

The amount paid by the Society during the past year for Death claims amounted to £5,867 15s.; for sickness £494 11s. 4d.; and for Endowments £513 13s. 6d. This last item speaks volumes for the forethought of the working classes and at a period like this when the Legislature are engaged in questions having for their avowed object the better protection and Education of the people facts like these tending to show what the working classes are capable of doing deserve attention at the hand of every person no matter what position in life he may be placed in.

The large amount paid by the Society to its Agents for the collection of Premiums may be brought against the Society by numerous persons and I will not say such persons are prejudiced but it must be borne in mind that this Society is purely an Industrial Office and the percentage paid in contra distinction to the amount paid by better class Offices is not an excessive rate of remuneration to Agents and when taken into consideration with its contingencies it will bear very favourable comparison with the rates paid by better class Offices.

The number of Agents at the close of the year 1870 was 126; the Directors during the year 1871 appointed 73 new agents and the present number of agents is 197.

The total number of Policies now existing is 51,376 and the Premiums amount to nearly £15,000 per annum and are daily increasing.

The steady progress of the Society reflects great credit on the Directors officers and agents and the resolution of the Directors not to dispute any Policy on any ground whatever except FRAUD commands itself to the Shareholders, Policyholders and the public generally.

The assets of the Society are in a highly satisfactory state.

(Signed) THOS. JOSH. C. L. BORDMAN, LL.D.
London.   February 17th, 1872

At this moment of time, with success long achieved, it is possible to look back sympathetically on what those assets really were:

Value of Property	£1,195	10	0
Promissory Notes and Bills of Exchange ..	359	14	0
Agents' Balances	460	13	7
Share capital not called up on 1,917 shares allotted	2,211	0	0
Cash in hand and on deposit	869	17	3
Total:	£5,096	14	10

The period from 1870 to the turn of the century was possibly the most important in the whole history of the Refuge. It was in these decades that the foundations on which to-day's business is built were consolidated. There were several reasons for this, both external and internal. There is little doubt that the 1870 Act put life assurance on the map; from then on it had, in the view of the public, Parliamentary backing and new business was on that account facilitated. Again, the statutory returns and the publicity accorded them most certainly put boards and managements on inquiry and resulted in a more professional approach to the business. Finally, the provision which required that any new life assurance company should deposit £20,000 with the Accountant-General prevented the repetition of the mushroom growths of the past, with a consequent reduction in the competition from weaker, and sometimes unscrupulous concerns. The established offices were thus enabled the better to build up their resources, and certainly that is what the Refuge did.

From that year the company progressed steadily towards its objective of real financial solidity. The policyholders' funds were gradually built up; the agency force was expanded; new business increased in a remarkable way; and sickness insurance was at last left behind, albeit with a legacy of over 70 years of future loss—happily small.

Most particularly, the ordinary branch of the business really began to take hold. This was the department which was to show phenomenal growth, so much so that it eventually equalled the industrial branch from which it took its rise. The two branches were in fact separated on December 31st, 1887, when out of a total of £179,415 of assets, £10,204 was transferred to the ordinary branch to form the life assurance fund, the remainder, consisting of £50,000 shareholders' capital and £119,211 life assurance fund, appearing in the industrial branch accounts. As a matter of interest the corresponding life assurance funds at the end of 1957 were:

| Ordinary branch | .. | .. | .. | £70,882,414 |
| Industrial branch | .. | .. | .. | £66,481,670 |

In 1876 the first financial investigation was made by the "actuary" as provided by the Act. The basic figures had by then become of a significant magnitude, the number of policies valued being 177,405, with a premium income of £51,701 per annum; each of these figures being about 3½ times as great as those of five years earlier. The valuation balance sheet is impressive, though in a negative sort of way: for it shows assurance funds amounting to £17,011, with a liability of " Nil ", and a surplus of £17,011. In fact, this sum was not regarded in any way as profit—as indeed it was not: and it was retained intact in the funds as a further step in that long process already referred to of strengthening the valuation reserves of the company.

Mr. Bordman's report in respect of this year is not in the records—which is a pity, for his style is distinctly original. He valued the office ten years later in 1886, when his valuation balance sheet gives evidence of a considerable improvement, the surplus shown being £65,243. His report for the succeeding year opens with the following flowing paragraph:

To the Policyholders:

" Life Assurance can well be described as one of the noblest monuments ever erected by enlightened humanity. The merits, the advantages and the general influence of Life Assurance are beyond doubt unparalleled. The arrangement to assure, and periodical payment of premiums is so eminently practical, rational, easy and just, that it is only to be regretted the practice is not far more general than it is among all classes of the community."

Reports to-day are dull by comparison.

In the first half of the company's history there are gaps in the records, and one of these occurs in the period 1869-72. It was during these three years that one of the founders, and two of the early pioneers, all of whom were directors, " disappeared ". They were George Robins, who from the beginning had carried the burden of secretary-ship, and who had so often extended financial help to the office in time

47

of need: and his later colleagues, J. H. Ferrand and George Bridge, the latter of whom was appointed treasurer in place of Joe Robins, and who also followed the example of the Robins brothers in advancing money from time to time. There is no record of what happened to his office-within-an-office, the Pim Hole Club: but no doubt the board honoured their agreement to carry on the arrangement for the benefit of his heirs until 1878, when their undertaking came to an end. It is to be assumed that all three died in harness; at all events by the end of 1872, their names had vanished from the minutes and others had taken their place.

On February 10th, 1872, three new directors were appointed out of seven individuals who were eligible for election to the board. The successful candidates were Henry Thornton, Henry Adams and Henry Bridge, Wm. Proctor being re-elected. Two weeks later, on February 24th, 1872, James Proctor was elected managing director of the company. This was to be the highest position he occupied: he was to be content to sit under his own son, Wm. Proctor, who became chairman in 1884. It seems typical of the man to avoid the limelight: yet as the detailed history of the Refuge is considered, even from the dates of the various deliberations before the original society was founded, it becomes more and more clear that the real driving force and dominant personality belonged to him. He saw clearly where the society properly belonged—to Manchester and thence outward: but he saw, too, where his own future lay—with his company, also in Manchester. That is quite certainly the reason which caused him to leave Preston and come to Livesey Street, a much more central spot from which to administer the business in Lancashire which had been entrusted to him as a director controlling an area.

He had a very high ideal of what an assurance man should be: and this he embodied in a letter which he sent to every new man appointed to the Staff. So fundamentally true is this message that even to-day a copy of it under the title: " A Letter from the Past for the Present and for the Future " is given to every new man on the outside staff. It reads as follows:

Refuge Assurance Company, Limited,
Manchester.

Dear Sir,

As you have been appointed by our company allow me to congratulate you, to give you a cordial greeting, and wish you every success in your work. It is my earnest desire that every one should be successful in his work, and earn enough to make himself comfortable in life, and easy and happy in the service of the company. Let me, therefore, ask your attention to the following particulars, as embodying in a few words the conditions of success.

1. HAVE CONFIDENCE IN YOUR CALLING AS AN HONOURABLE PROFESSION. Never be ashamed to have it known that you are an assurance representative. There are callings of which their representatives have cause to be ashamed, but the work of inducing persons to assure their lives is not one of them. Cheer yourself with daily remembrance that your work is to induce persons to be frugal, self-reliant, and independent.

2. RESOLVE THAT YOU WILL SUCCEED. Let this be the underground basis of all your actions, so that the office shall know that it has in you one who means to do its work, to serve its interests and deserve its confidence.

3. MIND YOUR BUSINESS by keeping your work always before you, and giving six days a week continuous attention to it. Do not think of having a gentleman's life, or you had better not begin your work. We do not want gentlemen in the sense of idlers—but workers. It is a proper law in this world, that if a man will not work he shall not succeed. Do not try to answer this remark by referring to some person who is an exception to it, for it will not serve you to follow exceptions. The rule is work and live, act on this rule and you will live. The office will trust you if it finds you always at work, and it will not trust you in any dodging which you may adopt in the place of work.

4. MAKE YOURSELF WELL ACQUAINTED WITH YOUR BUSINESS, so as to know its tables and the principles on which life assurance is based. In getting this information begin at the beginning, and so find your way gradually into the depths of the subject. Make a note of anything that arises which shows you your ignorance, or about which you are in doubt, and search it out on the first opportunity afterwards. By observation and care you will be astonished how soon you will gain the mastery of the subject.

5. GET YOUR WORK INTO ORDER, AND METHOD, AND PLACE, so as to work by system. Random effort can compete in no employment with

orderly effort.   This will form itself best in your work, you will not be able to make a plan first and bring it to your work and fit your work to it, for you may find the conditions of your work very different from what you supposed before you began.   Go to work and gradually reduce things to order and method, so as to work by system. Have a plan of your district, locate yourself as near to it as possible, all things being considered, and so work it as never to go over ground twice where once might have done as well.   Never find yourself saying " Dear me!   I have this to go over again. My head will never save my feet, or hands, or time ".

6.   VISIT ALL THE FAMILIES IN YOUR DISTRICT, and make yourself thoroughly acquainted with them.   Be kindly and courteous with everybody.   If any are not in a good mood, leave them with a kindly word and an agreeable smile, and see them again as soon as convenient, for they are likely to be ashamed if they have been rude or offensive, or even outdone in courtesy, and make ready to assure with you as a vindication of themselves.   In this way go through and round your district until your knowledge of it is complete for your purpose, and you may have become the acquaintance and friend of hundreds.   Why should you not have your parish as well as the clergyman, the doctor and other public servants in the district, in which you may secure a home for life, with a certain and ever-increasing income in return for your devotion to your work and service to the public?

7.   TRY TO INDUCE EVERY PERSON TO ASSURE.   Take a proposal for the least possible amount where you cannot get a larger sum, and then follow it up as prudently as you can to get it increased to a larger sum.   There are few persons who assure as much as they can, or as they ought, and there are fewer still whose first assurance is as large as they may be induced to make it.   Having constant intercourse with families it will be easy for you to see where their assurance can be increased with ease and safety to themselves, and, in such cases, openings will present themselves when you can effectively put in a word that may lead to its being increased.   When you get any person in the right line, follow it up unceasingly till the policy is effected. On the other hand, avoid being considered a bore to anyone, and on the other hand, equally avoid being considered indifferent.

8.   CULTIVATE CANDOUR in your intercourse with your policyholders, and impress them with a sense of your honesty and straightforward business character. When any other office is spoken of treat it with respect.

9.   If any life is offered you which you are certain is bad, kindly but firmly decline it, and if any policyholder inquire the reason show them that it is in their interest, as well as in the interest in the office, and that only good lives should be taken. By such conduct as this you will build up a reputation which, in the course of years,

will be worth a fortune to you, and make you worthy of the confidence of the office you represent.

10. BE REGULAR AND PUNCTUAL IN YOUR HABITS, and especially in your attention to business.   As far as possible collect the regular weekly premiums at the same moment from week to week, so that every one will learn to know, not only the certainty of your coming, but also the exact time.   This will so act upon them as to give them confidence in you, secure the regular payment of their premium, and so avoid lapses and the consequent loss of business.   It will also induce them to have the money ready, so as to enable you to collect twice the amount in the same time you would otherwise be able to collect it.

Yet in going your regular rounds never seem to be in a fuss, or too hurried to give those with whom you have to do business a kindly word, or to express sympathy with any who may have affliction in the house, or suffering under any reverse of any kind. If you meet with anything very special after a suitable word on the subject, promise to call again as soon as you can, which you must be very careful to do, always keeping your word.

11. If any stimulus is wanted to encourage your effort, you will find it in the following considerations: Firstly, your own gains will be in proportion with the gains of your office.   The better you serve the company, the better you will serve yourself. The more persons you induce to invest their money for their own future benefit, the more you will profit from the harvest which you will thus reap.   In no sphere of labour is the heaven-given law more certain in its operations than in life assurance. " He that watereth others, himself shall be watered ".   Secondly, life assurance is entitled to the highest position in the estimation of the public which it is possible for you to give it.

No matter from what point of observation it is surveyed, it becomes the more deserving of confidence and respect the clearer it is seen.   Men of every rank and class only want to know it better in order to esteem it the more.   You have, therefore, no need to shrink from talking about it, and holding it up in the clear light of day, that it may be seen and understood.   And thirdly, as the office you represent has already taken its place in the front rank of the institutions of its class, you can go about your work with the utmost confidence in its future success and stability.

Your company, having established its character and position, asks you to give proof of your right to a place among its trusted representatives, who have helped to make it what it now is by unceasing activity in its service, and unswerving loyalty to its interests.

Yours faithfully,

JAMES PROCTOR.

51

From time to time there are references in the minutes to new or revised tables, usually in terms which suggest that one or two members of the committee had been instructed to think up something which might be advantageous to the office.   Thus, a director might be instructed to revise the scale of sickness benefit, which appeared to be too generous; or to alter the premium rates under one of the assurance tables; or " to get up a first-class table similar to Table C " (this last was an instruction to the secretary).   In this connection, there is a significant minute dated as late as August 4th, 1887:

> The Chairman introduced the subject of new tables so as to compete with other kindred Companies and Societies—a long discussion took place when it was resolved " that the chairman produce an ' Infantile and other tables ' to be submitted to next board meeting, and any member of the board to bring tables likewise to be submitted ".

It will be remembered that the Registrar, in certifying the establishment of the society, made a specific point of saying " the Rates of Contributing and payments are not stated to have been prepared by any Actuary ".   It is exceedingly unlikely that any actuary *had* been employed on such a task: the strong probability is that the rates of some similar office were copied, with or without some minor alterations for the sake of appearances, as was by no means an uncommon practice in those days.   Whether or not the Refuge sought the advice of Thos. Josh. Bordman as to the adequacy of the rates current at the date of his appointment is not known; probably they did, for the members of the committee were too businesslike not to get advice when it was available, and certainly as regards new tables it was usual to submit them to the actuary for approval or otherwise.

On October 25th, 1878, the company removed its head office once again.   Nothing is known as to what actually led up to this second move to 85-89 Corporation Street.   It is easy, and almost certainly correct to conclude that more room was needed.   The accounts show that the business was growing at a tremendous pace: that of itself

11/13 Corporation Street, Manchester

85/89 Corporation Street, Manchester

would mean more clerks, more records, more space required—and its corollary, room to expand again. Of the search for the new premises, and the shortcomings of the old offices at Nos. 11-13, we know nothing.

It is known that the same landlord owned both properties, and that there was more room in the new offices than in the old. The former stood on what was—and still is—virtually an island site, the frontage being Corporation Street, the rear being Long Millgate, in which stands Victoria Station. On the two sides stood two well-known hostelries, the Manchester Arms and the Bay Horse Inn: there they stand to-day, after seventy years. Years before, when the office was in Dukinfield in 1862, the committee of management decided

" that William Bradburn be allowed for providing Refreshments for Agents or any other Officer of the Society that comes on business to the office ".

Which of the committee was responsible for this sociable idea is not apparent, though it is perhaps not a bad guess that it was Bradburn himself: thus providing a combination of business and pleasure, or as someone once put it, an attractive association of office and snug. In any event, following Bradburn's resignation, a minute was passed on rather a bleak note:

" That no expenses be allowed in treating agents only where desirable and cannot be avoided ".

Had the practice continued, how refreshingly, as it were, would the facilities at 85-89 Corporation Street have appealed to the originator of the idea and his visitors !

The move was probably only a temporary one, for the lease was for but seven years. In 1884, the directors began seriously to seek for a home that would, as far as could humanly be judged, be permanent. This was a serious problem which took a long time and many arguments to solve: and indeed the company had to remain in Corporation Street for eleven more years before making its final move to the present offices in Oxford Street.

This chapter may well close with the recording of a resolution passed at a special meeting of shareholders on September 2nd, 1881:

" That the name of the company shall be changed to Refuge Assurance Company Limited ".

The change of name brought no alteration whatever in the status of the company. It remained, as before, subject to the provisions of the Life Assurance Companies Act, 1870. It had left the shelter—and possible disadvantages—of the Friendly Societies Act far behind in 1864, when it became incorporated as a limited liability company. What then prompted the change? It is only possible to-day to speculate; but it seems probable that the board was anxious to remove the words " Friendly Society " from its title.

The friendly society movement was going through a bad patch in the 'seventies and 'eighties. There were a number of old-established and honourable friendly societies in existence—the Manchester Unity of Oddfellows, the Ancient Order of Foresters, and the like. There were a number of collecting friendly societies getting into their stride after an existence of 20 or 30 years—the Royal Liver, the Liverpool Victoria, and so on. But equally, among the many smaller friendly societies, often local in character, there were a number which tottered on the brink of disaster year after year and often collapsed eventually with loss and distress to their members. It may well be that, established and flourishing as the Refuge then was, in particular with the prospect of a rapidly growing ordinary branch, the board concluded that it was time to break with a style that was not only becoming a misnomer but which appeared to associate the office with a movement which was then under active criticism. So enters the Refuge Assurance Company, Limited.

CHAPTER VII

Rapid Expansion

THE new-styled company set out on its career with the impetus behind it of a premium income increasing at a most impressive rate. It has been recorded earlier that in 1871 the combined premium income was nearly £15,000—in fact £14,457. By 1881 it was £121,349, an increase in ten years of £106,892, a remarkable record by any standard. There were two main reasons for this success. Britain herself was growing, and the management of the Refuge was in the hands of men ready to see and to seize every opportunity of furthering the company, and prepared to work without stint in its interests.

The Refuge was fortunately situated in the heart of an increasingly busy industrial area. In and around Manchester there were in 1850 a quarter of a million cotton mill employees; yet the district was to be outstripped in production by the neighbouring Bolton, Oldham, Rochdale and Blackburn areas. It became the entrepôt city for the teeming production of Lancashire and Yorkshire. Small wonder that the chairman and secretary were authorised to sign on behalf of the company the monster petition which was organised in favour of building the Manchester Ship Canal, which when opened in 1895 was to lift Manchester from an inland textile centre to the third largest seaport in the country.

This was a fertile field for the company to cultivate and it did so with great effect. It is not surprising that the new offices in Corpora-

55

tion Street were becoming quite impossible for the housing of the rapidly growing mountain of day-to-day paper work, the storage of documents and stationery, and the accommodation of the staff essential for dealing with it all. But by that time the search for new and permanent premises was already in hand.

In 1884 an extraordinary general meeting was held to make substantial additions to the board, and to replace James Woodcock, who died about that time. Those elected were Thos. Shutt, Jas. Proctor (Junior), Wm. Adams, James Wilcock; and Robert Moss, the clerk who had been taken into the office in Dukinfield in 1862. A week later the board elected its first permanent chairman. From the very earliest days of the original society no one had, in fact, held this position: meetings of every kind, whether committee, board, general, extraordinary, had each been presided over by a chairman appointed *ad hoc*, various members of the managing body performing the duty at different times. For many years preceding his death, James Woodcock more often than not occupied the position: but the system can hardly have been satisfactory. Accordingly, by a majority vote—which included that of his father, James—Wm. Proctor was elected to the post, which he was to hold until his death fourteen years later. His father retained his position as managing director.

The new director, Robert Moss, was appointed secretary, and a stout effort was made to have a treasurer appointed. This was defeated by the narrowest of margins. It seems to have been rather an unnecessary suggestion: for although since the death of the first and only other secretary, George Robins, minutes of meetings had been taken by Henry Bridge, they appear to have been copied out again and entered in Moss's beautiful copper-plate: whilst when a month later Moss's duties as secretary were set out in detail and the appropriate resolution approved, they included everything a treasurer might have been expected to do—and omitted only the obvious task of a secretary, the recording of the minutes of meetings! As defining his job this

56

lengthy resolution must have given Moss some satisfaction, and he probably entered it in the minute book with amusement. He had been performing all those tasks for years.

It was in this year, 1884, that the capital of the company was increased from £50,000 to £100,000, still divided into shares of £2 each. The subscriptions in respect of the new share capital were charged in the years 1890 and 1891 at the rate of £25,000 in each year, making the paid-up capital £100,000 on December 31st, 1891. Not at all a bad development of the £22 12s. 6d. capital upon which the Friend in Deed began operations 33 years before.

It is interesting to observe how the management of the office began to assume a standard form. Under the system of directors' districts, conditions might vary as between one and the other, including remuneration to collectors and even rates of premium. Among the alterations which gradually appeared in the interest of uniformity, there was in 1885 a general streamlining of terms and conditions for all servants of the company from directors downwards. In the earlier days, area supervisors were given " times " and commission out of which they paid the agents and collectors. New terms were now arranged for directors who were area supervisors, and it was resolved on October 22nd, 1885

" that all canvassers, agents, assistants, and supers engaged by or for the company after this date be appointed upon one uniform system of remuneration and that with due regard to previous contracts and the present unduly large expenses and small savings of the company the same system shall apply as far as possible to those already engaged ".

It was a move nicely calculated not only to facilitate the clerical work at chief office, but also to define and raise the status of the field man. With the prevailing mixture of full and part-time agents something of this sort was highly desirable: and a further step in raising the standard in the field force was the adoption of a bond form for agents. The very fact that an agent could obtain a bond was evidence of his good standing: and since the agent through his intimate contact with the public has always been regarded as the company's best advertisement, it was naturally wise to be careful in the choice of the hands in which the Refuge reputation might lie.

A second step towards mechanisation may give rise to an understanding smile. In June, 1886, the board resolved unanimously " that a telephone be put on to chief office." It may not sound important in this age of the electronic computer, but in those days it represented progress indeed.

In a previous chapter, rather anticipating events, reference was made to the separation of the two branches, the industrial and the ordinary, at the end of 1887: and also to the search set on foot in 1884 for a site for a new and permanent chief office. The next event in point of time to be mentioned is one which mattered enormously to the company: the passing in 1888 of that most significant, enterprising, yet modest figure, James Proctor. His death in February was a personal blow to all his colleagues on the board. They undoubtedly felt a real sense of loss at the passing of a man, as they wrote in a letter of condolence to his widow in terms which were genuinely sincere— " to whom we have been able to look up for counsel and guidance, and especially as he was the last survivor of its promoters who has stood by the Company in all its trials and witnessed its unparalleled prosperity ". No greater tribute to the man can be paid than to say that his death did not affect the fortunes of the company. In fact, he had achieved that most difficult of things—he had made himself dispensable. He had so guided the superintendent-directors over the years, and with the aid of Robert Moss had created such an efficient administrative centre at chief office, that the Refuge machine went on, unimpeded by the absence of the man who was in so great a degree its creator.

William Proctor was appointed manager in the place of his father, in addition to remaining chairman. The reaction in the industrial assurance world to the death of James and the appointment of his son is to be noted, oddly enough, in a letter from another company with whom the Refuge had been in disagreement. The managing director wrote:

" . . . Personally, I may say that the shock I experienced on hearing of the death of your lamented father, for whom I had an intense respect, killed all my hard feelings, and I would have liked to have sent my sympathy with you but I was afraid I might have been misunderstood.

" I shall, however, be glad to let the past be dead and sign an agreement: and I shall loyally abide by it in every form when signed. . . .

" If not out of place I would like to add my congratulations to you on your appointment as manager to the company you have done so much to bring to its present proud position."

Perhaps the greatest difficulty confronting all industrial assurance companies and societies from the earliest days in the 'fifties was the intense competition that developed amongst their outside representatives. It has been said earlier that the agent of the new-style industrial assurance office was feared competitively, and consequently cordially disliked by the representatives of the local friendly and burial societies and other collecting clubs on whose ground he was encroaching. Those were pretty uninhibited days: and may well be summed up in the words of a very successful field man who said, speaking of his early agency days in a very rough area, " My Sundays with the Salvation Army were often exciting: but no more than my weekdays when trying to collect my premiums before someone else got them ".

The struggle for new business led to the growth of a most undesirable practice known as " transferring ". A transfer, as we understand it to-day, means the transferring of the name and existing policies of a policyholder from one agent's book to that of another agent in the same office, usually when the policyholder removes from one district to another. In the later years of the 1800's it meant transferring from one office to another.

This was a practice which became rife, and whether they intended it or no, the Refuge and particularly its employees were forced to engage in it. There is evidence to show that the committee was alive to the fact that there was little future for a business built on such shifting sands as a floating membership. The urgent need was for stability, and this was certainly not encouraged by collectors from other offices inducing the policyholders to drop their Refuge contracts and take out new ones with the poaching concern—with the inevitable and very human result of retaliation by the collector whose business was interfered with. From the point of view of the policyholder it would probably appear to him that his position would be affected only by a change in the collector, as the new policy would be issued " without loss of benefit ", i.e., entitled to immediate full benefit without the customary waiting period, if it was so entitled in the original society; whilst if another birthday had not been passed the sum assured for a given premium might well remain unaltered. But the more usual result was that the new assurance was begun at a later age, and must therefore be paid for at a higher rate.

The more important societies were, like the Refuge, opposed to the practice, as a matter of good business sense: but with the scattered nature of the debits and the almost impossibility of ensuring that new policies were not, in fact, " transferred policies ", the different head offices were in a great difficulty. The most they could do was to enter into agreements with one another not to take each other's collectors and members, and one such was made with the Liverpool Victoria in 1866. This was a real attempt at management level to stop the evils of transferring, of substituting policies, of poaching staff, and of denigration—of which there are frequent instances in the company's records, when the Refuge and its collectors were abused and maligned by the men of other offices: to all of which there is not the slightest doubt that the Refuge men replied in full measure. It has to be admitted that it must have been very galling to have these damaging falsehoods circulating in one's area, sometimes even in the form of a printed and entirely anonymous circular: but this free-for-all war of

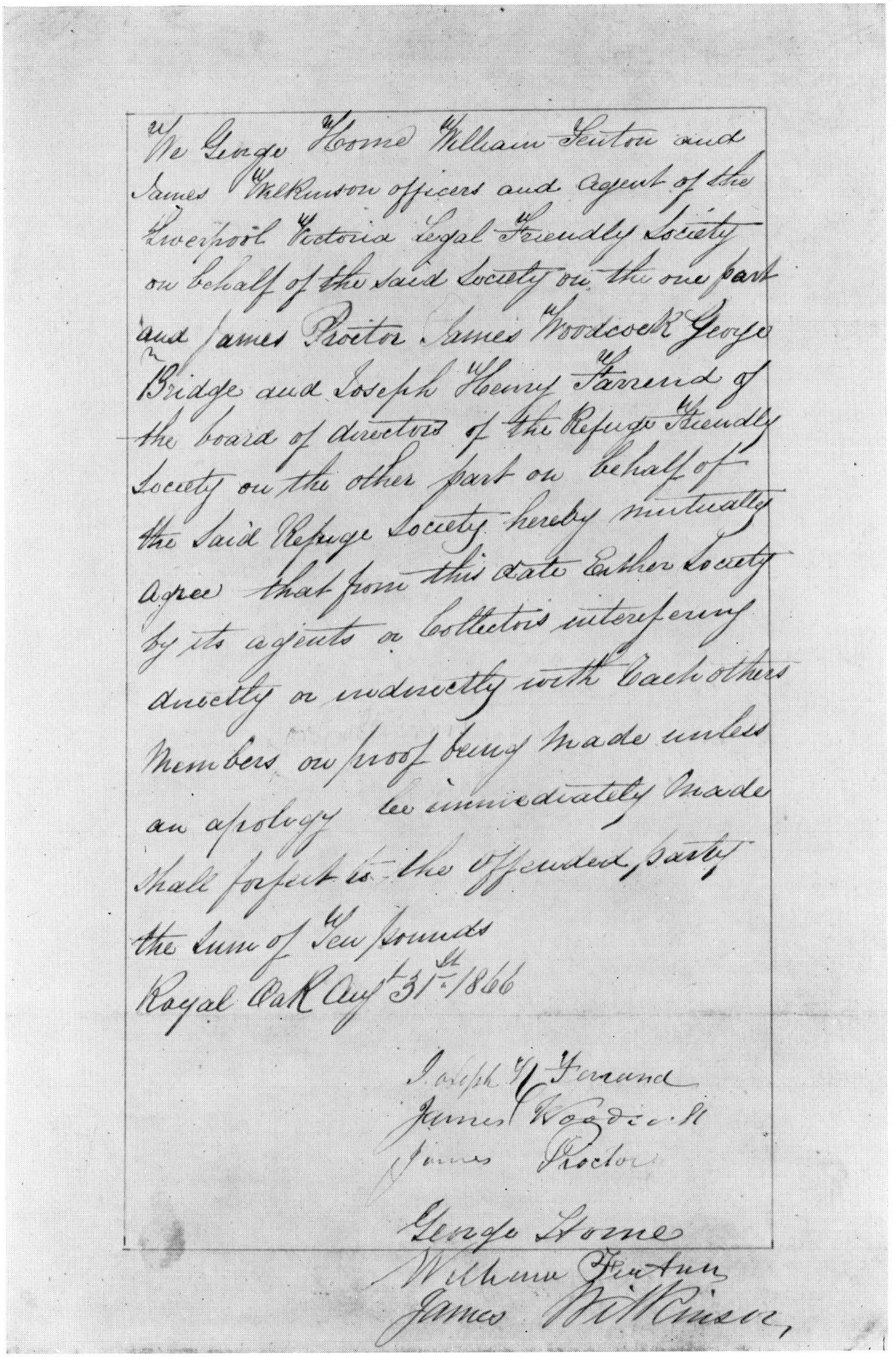

We George Home William Fenton and James Wilkinson officers and agent of the Liverpool Victoria Legal Friendly Society on behalf of the said Society on the one part and James Proctor James Woodcock George Bridge and Joseph Henry Townend of the board of directors of the Refuge Friendly Society on the other part on behalf of the said Refuge Society hereby mutually agree that from this date Either Society by its agents or collectors interfering directly or indirectly with Each others Members on proof being made unless an apology be immediately made shall forfeit to the offended party the Sum of Ten pounds

Royal Oak Augt 31st 1866

Joseph H Townend
James Woodcock
James Proctor

George Home
William Fenton
James Wilkinson,

Agreement with Liverpool Victoria Legal Friendly Society

No. 1 Building, Oxford Street
(from a water colour by Alfred Waterhouse, R.A.)

words was obviously a bad thing, and although it took a long time, it was eventually made to cease.

The agreement with the Liverpool Victoria was apparently the first, to be followed by another with the Pearl in 1883. There are records of these agreements being renewed from time to time and it appears too, that similar arrangements were made with other offices as occasion arose.

The agreement with the Pearl, of which a copy is fortunately extant, sums up the whole difficulty, and makes it quite clear that both offices were aware of the undesirability of the practice and resolved to end it. It reads as follows:

NOTICE

To the Agents, Collectors, and Canvassers of the PEARL LIFE ASSURANCE COMPANY, LIMITED, and the REFUGE ASSURANCE COMPANY, LIMITED.

The Directors of the above Companies having entered into a Covenant for the *effectual suppression of transferring policyholders*, do hereby give Notice that from and after this date the following Regulations will be strictly enforced:

1. No Agent, Collector, Canvasser or other person filling any office of trust in connection with the Refuge Assurance Company, Limited, shall by any means induce any Agent, Collector, Canvasser, or other servant, or any policyholder or policyholders of the Pearl Life Assurance Company, Limited, to leave that company and join the Refuge Assurance Company, Limited; nor shall any Agent, Collector, Canvasser, or other person filling any office of trust in connection with the Pearl Life Assurance Company, Limited, induce any Agent, Collector, Canvasser, or other responsible servant, or policyholder or policyholders of the Refuge Assurance Company, Limited, to leave that Company and join the Pearl Life Assurance Company, Limited; nor shall any Agent, Collector, Canvasser, or other servant of either company, make any statement or representation to the policyholders of the other Company calculated to bring discredit upon, or render such policyholders dissatisfied with the Company to which they respectively belong, in the event of so doing he shall be compelled to go to the residence of such policyholder with a representative of the Company that such policyholder has been induced to leave, and

return any money or document he may have taken or received from such policy-holder, and will be expected to apologise in the presence of the persons complaining.

2. That no Agent, Collector, or Canvasser who has been employed by either Company shall be employed by the other, unless satisfactory references have been received from the Manager of the Company by whom such Agent, Collector, or Canvasser, was formerly employed.

3. Should any person obtain employment in any capacity in either of the said Companies by means of false representations, such person shall be discharged immediately, providing such discovery be made within a period of six months from the time when he obtained such employment by means of such false representation as aforesaid, and if such discovery shall be made after the period of six months, he shall be dealt with as the directors of the said companies shall determine.

4. And whereas the foregoing regulations are intended solely for the mutual protection of the said companies and their policyholders against the evil practice of transferring, and in the interest of all parties concerned, we therefore desire that a cordial and friendly feeling be cultivated amongst the various servants of the said companies.

Signed on behalf of the directors of the Pearl Life Assurance Company, Limited.

P. J. FOLEY, *Manager.*

Signed on behalf of the directors of the Refuge Assurance Company, Limited.

JAMES PROCTOR, *Manager.*

September 29th, 1883

Amended Agreement in Place of the One Formerly in Force.

This was an achievement which was not only worth while in itself, but which showed remarkable prescience, for the objects which it set forth were a substantial part of the aims of the Association of Industrial Assurance Companies and Collecting Friendly Societies which was to be born in 1901, as will later be seen.

What was probably then regarded as a minor improvement, but which proved later to be of great importance, was the cancellation of the old contribution card and its substitution by a premium receipt book. This was brought out in July, 1887, and was a success from the start. Including as it did pages covering a period of several years, divided into weekly or monthly periods, it had the psychological effect of suggesting the permanency of the policies and the stability of the company. With the record of weeks and months and years of premium payments in front of him a policyholder did not so readily contemplate letting his policies lapse as when he had merely a small card containing up to a mere twelve months' payments. This was not an original idea on the part of the Refuge, for the British Industry, the first industrial assurance company, had used such a premium book 35 years before. Probably the Refuge had been precluded from adopting the notion by the higher cost involved. It is interesting to observe that throughout the business this form of record of premiums paid very early became common form, and has remained practically unaltered from that day to this.

About 1888, two questions were exercising the minds of the directors—a permanent chief office, and a qualified actuary. The former had indeed been a source of worry for some years; several properties being considered, a great deal of argument taking place at board meetings, decisions being taken—and almost immediately reversed. The first idea was to buy and extend the existing premises in Corporation Street: the next one involved buildings in Peter Street: next came property in Halliwell Lane as to which opinion, though divided, was in favour. Nevertheless, whether the property was bought or not, the chief office did not go there. Instead, the existing lease was extended, later " the house at the back " was added and the company settled again, though doubtless in a state of sad congestion.

That was to be the end of making do, for there was no other property which could conveniently be added to the existing premises. What the directors were now after was a site on which to build and later to expand.

A block at the corner of Deansgate and Peter Street was not only considered, but very nearly purchased: suddenly the whole deal collapsed, possibly because word had gone round that the present site at the corner of Oxford Street and Whitworth Street was to come on the market. Wm. Proctor was given *carte blanche* to secure the land and report to the board who, on September 29th, 1890, were unanimous in the purchase

" of a piece of Freehold Land containing 45 yards of frontage in Oxford Street and 40 yards in Whitworth Street in all 1,800 yards square for the sum of £21,000 less £2,000 allowed for payment of Chief Rent of £80 per annum ".

There is a touch of sentiment in the thought that the fine new buildings to be erected on this site to form the company's chief office were to be only five minutes' walk from George Robins' little house at 15 Hart Street, where the original society had its first home nearly forty years before.

The company engaged Alfred Waterhouse R.A., architect of the Manchester Town Hall, to design the new building, and within a surprisingly short span of time his plans were laid before the directors in January, 1891. For a board composed of men of strong personality and quite definitely with wills of their own there was a remarkable unanimity concerning Waterhouse's proposals:

" Resolved unanimously that the Six plans of the floors of the new offices produced be accepted ".

The only suggestion which was ventured—and adopted—was:

" that the words to be placed in Terra Cotta on front of the building be as follows, viz: Refuge Assurance Company, Ltd."

It took four and a half years for the building to be ready for occupation, a period which must have caused headaches as well as the excitement of anticipation. Yet the only mention of the building in all that time in the directors' minute book was " Messrs. Sothern's Tender (yellow pine woodwork) for building the Superstructure of the New Chief Office be accepted ".

Presumably the architect fully earned his fee and shouldered every problem which occurred. Even the opening of the building went almost unnoticed. The only record is a minute of the board meeting on July 25th, 1895, that " several matters were brought forward and discussed, but no resolutions taken thereon—afterwards short sayings relative to the improvement of the new offices over the old ones ".

The buildings were of advanced design and in being spacious, light and airy were in marked contrast to the old offices in Corporation Street. There was room and to spare for staff and stuff—a most refreshing change: and yet within a mere ten years, the company was to begin to build its first extension.

The second pre-occupation of the board towards the end of the 1880's was whether or not to appoint a qualified actuary: and if so, whom. The company was by now heading for very large figures: and since the number of actuaries fully qualified by examination was not now so small as to render it almost impossible to find one, the board felt that it was only proper that they should avail themselves of the services of a Fellow of the Institute or Faculty of Actuaries. They did in fact decide to approach a well-known actuary of the period, with a view to ascertaining whether he was open to an appointment with the company and upon what terms. Nothing came of it, however: and indeed it was unlikely anything would, as circumstances then were in the professional field. Much the better notion was, if possible, to find an actuarial student well on in his examinations who could join the company, complete his fellowship, and thereafter be appointed actuary to the Refuge. Such a prospect was actually on the doorstep of the company in the person of a young man by the name of W. H. Aldcroft who was working in the branch office in Manchester of another life assurance company. In those days the examinations were in three parts; the passing of parts 1 and 2 gave the candidate his Associateship, and part 3 his Fellowship. Aldcroft had passed part 1 in 1888 and part 2 in 1890 and by doing so had become an A.I.A.; but more than that— he had done so without working in the head office of a life assurance company, where only could be found the practical application of actuarial science. He was just the man for the Refuge, and he joined the staff in 1891. He completed his fellowship in 1894, was appointed actuary in 1896, and was later to become general manager, and finally a director.

The next financial investigation pursuant to the 1870 Act was made in 1891, the end of the quinquennium since 1886. On the directors' instructions, the newly joined Aldcroft invited the well-known actuary, Mr. James Chatham, to value the young ordinary branch, which had only been in existence four years, and contained a large proportion of with-profit business in respect of which nine-tenths of the divisible profits were to be distributed to the policyholders by way of a reversionary bonus. As a result of his valuation, a reversionary bonus was declared at the rate of £1 2s. 6d. per cent. on the sum assured under participating policies—the first bonus of its type in the history of the company.

The valuation of the industrial branch was once again made by Thos. Josh Bordman; but this occasion was his last, though his name appears in the balance sheet for 1892, curiously enough for the first and only time using the simple initials T.J.C.L. He died some time after he signed this document, which is dated February 27th, 1893.

W. H. Aldcroft's first valuation was made in respect of the quinquennium ending December 31st, 1896. Henceforth, valuations were to be made annually, with annual declarations of reversionary bonus in the ordinary branch. The bonus declared on this occasion was at the rate of £1 6s. per cent. on the sum assured. His valuation of the industrial branch was distinguished by a significant strengthening of the valuation basis: from now on this process was to be continued as part of a systematic campaign to build up the company's financial resources.

The century closed on a depressing note for the office. In 1893 it had to deal with the difficulties consequent on the cotton strike and the coal lock-out, and to meet the financial strain due to the influenza epidemic of that year. Two years later the directors made special mention in their report of the serious effect of a recurrence of this same epidemic. Later on the South African war broke out: and finally at the end of 1898 the death occurred of William Proctor, the first permanent Chairman and General Manager. He had been an able member of the Board, and a most capable manager: the Company had grown impressively under his control.

It is not known when William first joined the Company: but most probably he began to work in his father's Director-Area immediately upon leaving school, an experience—under such a preceptor—which would account for his detailed knowledge of the business in all its aspects. Certainly his ability must have been considerable, for it was no light matter to combine the offices of Chairman and General Manager—a unique distinction—in those exciting years. He had set a high standard for his successors.

The new Chairman was James Wilcock, the man who, thirty years before, had been appointed district manager for Blackburn at the age of 22, with a total staff of two part-time agents.

CHAPTER VIII

Legislation

SOUTH AFRICAN WAR: ASSOCIATION OF INDUSTRIAL ASSURANCE
COMPANIES AND COLLECTING FRIENDLY SOCIETIES: STAFF
ORGANISATION: LIFE ASSURANCE COMPANIES ACT, 1909:
NATIONAL HEALTH INSURANCE: DEATH OF JAMES WILCOCK:
FIRST RESIDENT SOLICITOR: OPENING OF NO. 2 BUILDING.

ALTHOUGH the outbreak of the war in South Africa did not materially affect the welfare of the company, it was nevertheless a most significant event, not only to the country as a whole, but to every individual part of it, of which the Refuge was one. The board did not realise—how could they?—that it was the comparatively insignificant forerunner of greater troubles to come: but it is to be recorded that the attitude they adopted towards those of their employees who served in the Forces, and to those of their policyholders who fell in the war, was to be repeated a bare fourteen years ahead: and yet again within a further twenty-five years. It all sounds sadly familiar; it was resolved unanimously

" that the Company pay in full the claims under Policies on the lives of persons killed in the present war in South Africa without charging any premium to cover war risks or any extra premium whatever ".

And again

" that a letter be sent to all the Superintendents asking for information relative to any Agent that may have been called out to serve with the Army in South Africa and if the Joint Managers are satisfied that there is a case for an allowance to be made for the benefit of the wife and children to grant such sums per week as they think will meet the case ".

Another resolution which fortunately did not need to be repeated

68

Philip Smith

JAMES S. PROCTOR

on the outbreak of the later wars, was that " the Company subscribe a hundred guineas to the Manchester, Salford and District South African Fund for the relief of Wives, Widows and Children of Soldiers engaged in the war in South Africa."

Although a number of the staff, both at chief office and in the field, either volunteered for service, or, being reservists, were recalled to the Colours, it is unlikely that the company was called upon to shoulder any sums of moment on their account. Among the agents, 32 are recorded as " Army " or " Army Reserve " and 14 as " Gone to South Africa ": whilst in the group, " clerks, assistants and officials ", 13 wives are shown to be in receipt of Army reserve allowance. British casualties in the three years of war were, by modern standards, insignificant, being 5,774 died in battle and 16,000 through disease: but there is no record of how many Refuge employees or policyholders were included in those figures. Probably the most serious effect on the company's finances was due to the influenza epidemics in 1899 and 1900, the claims through this cause alone in the industrial branch in the latter year being ten per cent. higher than might have been expected, representing an additional payment of some £40,000.

About this time industrial assurance had become a significant factor in the economic life in the country, over £11,000,000 being collected each year in premiums by the offices concerned. It was largely free from legislative control, and it was for the offices themselves to set the standard. For this purpose a meeting took place in 1901 of those engaged in the business, as a result of which the Association of Industrial Assurance Companies and Collecting Friendly Societies was formed with the objects of:

(a) The carrying out of any lawful thing which shall tend to promote the principles, practice and business of Industrial Assurance and for mutual protection against unfair or prejudicial legislation.

(b) The prevention as far as is practicable of what is known as
"transferring".

(c) The stoppage of the circulation of disparaging statements
against kindred Institutions or their representatives.

The association was remarkably successful in setting its house in
order, for within two years the honorary secretary was able to report
that "the undesirable state of things which prevailed prior to our
inauguration as an Association has to a large extent disappeared".
He was referring then to the two evils of "transferring" and "dis-
paragement"—both the product of uncontrolled competition between
the vigorous salesmen of the various offices, and both overcome by the
laying down of rules by the industry itself. The association has since
proved itself of great value in a wide field, and whenever action is
necessary for the industry as a whole it is this body to which reference
is made. It is now known as the Industrial Life Offices Association—
the I.L.O.A.

The Refuge has been closely connected with the association since
its formation, and has been represented officially by the undermen-
tioned:

Date of Appointment		Name	Position
1902	..	R. W. GREEN	Executive Member
1902	..	JOHN W. PROCTOR	Executive Member
1912	..	PHILIP SMITH	Executive Member
1922	..	J. PROCTOR GREEN	Executive Member 1928 Deputy-Chairman 1932 Vice-Chairman
1922	..	JAS. S. PROCTOR	Executive Member
1928	..	J. WILCOCK HOLGATE	Executive Member 1948 Vice-President

Date of Appointment		Name	Position
1945	..	WM. PROCTOR SMITH	Executive Member
1952	..	M. WILCOCK HOLGATE	Executive Member
			1955 Vice-Chairman
			1956 Chairman

In addition, the company's solicitor and actuary for the time being have continuously served on the legal or actuarial committees of the association.

In the opening years of the present century the organisation of the staff, both at chief office and in the field, was in a state of change. The old idea of a number of directors' areas, covering the whole of the company's business, autonomous in many respects, had been lost in the march of time. Directors' areas still remained: but no longer on a part-time basis, and no longer controlling the whole of the company's activities away from Manchester. Development had been too rapid for that: and there were many districts, new districts, which dealt directly with, and were administered by chief office. But not entirely.

The great merit of the system of directors' areas was that many decisions, of minor significance perhaps to the office but often enough of great importance in the eyes of the individuals concerned, could be taken by the man on the spot; who spent nearly all his time in the area and who would, often enough, know personally the people involved, sympathise with their idiosyncrasies, appreciate their standards of probity, and allow for the oddities of the district—who could, in a word, maintain that idea of personal attention implicit in the regular weekly calls of the collector. It was now sought to maintain this by grouping the collectors—henceforward to be styled agents—in districts under the control of a Superintendent, himself a former collector, the districts themselves being in turn grouped into divisions, each under the control of an inspector, himself a promoted superintendent. Within his area an inspector exercised considerable freedom of supervision, but the day-to-day work was carried on directly between his districts and chief office. In this respect he differed from a controlling director with whom his superintendents dealt direct.

The original director-areas were Manchester (James—afterwards William—Proctor); Blackburn (James Wilcock); Warrington (Henry Thornton); Sheffield (Henry Adams); to which was later added Liverpool (Thomas Shutt). Each director lived in his own area and only travelled to Manchester for board meetings or as occasion demanded. From his office, with his own clerical staff, he conducted his area almost as though it were an entity in itself, subject only to a measure of control by chief office in financial matters. He and his colleagues played an important part in the building up of the company: but with the growth of chief office as an increasingly efficient administrative centre, they gradually became outmoded, and in April, 1951, they were finally dispensed with.

As regards chief office, there is little in the records to indicate the number or the quality of the clerks engaged up to the turn of the century. One rather surprising fact emerges in the discovery that four lady clerks were engaged in the Corporation Street office as early as in 1874. And not only that; two of them continued to be employed, but now in Oxford Street, until the death of one in 1907, and the retirement on pension of the other the following year. Naturally, these four ladies were segregated from the males, as later were the lady clerks in the first Oxford Street building in 1895. In those days, although clerking was regarded as one of the genteel occupations a lady might follow should the necessity arose, certainly she could not work on a level footing with, and in the company of, males. Consequently, the new offices in Oxford Street contained on the top floor a department known for years as the " Harem ", cut off entirely from the rest of the office. The ladies arrived at the office after the men and left before them, thus being preserved from supposedly dangerous associations. They did not go out for lunch but cooked their own midday meals in a kitchen within the department and consumed them in their own refectory—which was really one of the attics. In this respect they were much better off than their male counterparts, who had no such dining space, and who in general either brought their own lunch with them, or sent the youngest recruit out to buy sardines, sandwiches, cake, fruit, and so on: always consumed at their desks, washed down by copious draughts of strong tea prepared for them by another junior; each in his special jug, from the " brew " brought in a screw of paper.

They seem to have been an enterprising and interesting collection of males—naturally perhaps, if another of the stories current in the chief office was true. According to this tale the accommodation in the new No. 1 building was so ample as to enable the management at last to employ a sufficient staff to deal with the impressive influx of new business: whereupon an official took his stand outside the office and asked every third man who passed " Would you like to be a clerk here? " And according to the legend quite a number of them did.

Actually, the recruitment of staff could not take place on the more systematic lines of the future by the engagement of clerks of school-leaving age. It is extremely probable that the office was growing so rapidly that there was no time to organise the staff and its engagement on such a long-term footing. Thus, on May 20th, 1895, a giant intake took place of 75 new lady clerks who formed the separate department to which reference has been made, and who were employed on policy-writing (later typing), card preparation and similar copying work under a supervisor, Miss Birchall; who held that position until her marriage in 1925 to Mr. Brand Lane, a famous figure in Manchester concert circles. The department was then broken up and its members and their work distributed throughout the office.

There was a celebrated period about 1896 when the whole of the actuarial department was on overtime for three years ($2\frac{1}{2}$ hours a night for 9d. tea money: it was never called overtime pay—in those days one

was expected to work as long as one was required).   It is also on record
that the staff involved carried out their task with complete cheerfulness
—as one old stager put it " Why not?   The boss worked as well ": as
indeed he did.

This happening was illustrative of the pressure of work the management had to worry about in those progressive and formative years: and
since in those less complicated days much of the work was purely
routine, men of any age could be, and in fact were, appointed to the
staff.   Naturally enough, this became quite a mixed collection: and
amongst them was a number of " characters " as seems always to be the
case whenever any sizeable body of men is gathered together.   Their
rate of pay, though up to the standard of the times, was not high; and—
this being an age of self-help—it was quite usual for them to have spare-
time occupations such as playing in theatre orchestras, running shorthand classes, acting for clothing clubs, helping in the family's little
shop, teaching in night schools, watch repairing, working overtime,
and so on.   It used to be said that a clerk could arrive in the morning
in the ordinary course of events and leave at night with a new suit, his
shoes re-soled, his watch repaired, money in his pocket, a meat-pie and
teacakes, and a reliable tip for the big race for the next day: having had
a shorthand lesson (3d. a time) and a haircut and shave: all off his
colleagues.

By the tenets of the modern systems of staff selection, it would
hardly be thought possible that so unstudied a system of recruitment
would produce good results.   Yet it did.   At no time since the advent
of W. H. Aldcroft in 1891 has the company made any importations,
other than that of M. Wilcock Holgate in 1946 as joint secretary, to
fill any of the higher official positions, which, with this exception, have
always been taken up by men already on the staff.   These were—
indeed, are—men who can be regarded as self-made in that they
studied long hours in their spare time to pass the examinations of a
number of professional bodies, such as the Institute or the Faculty of

74

Actuaries, the Law, the Chartered Insurance Institute, the Faculty of Insurance, the Institute of Secretaries, the University; or they studied, if not to pass examinations, then to make themselves so conversant with the practical aspects of the business as to enable them to fill most effectively the non-professional administrative positions. This breeding, as it were, of its own officials has long been a source of pride to the company.

In 1909 the Refuge, in common with all other life assurance or general insurance offices, came under the control of a new statute. Ever since the 1870's life assurance, as a whole, had been regulated by the Acts passed in that period: and later legislation by definition had distinguished between the industrial and the ordinary branches, the difference being that if premiums were receivable at intervals longer than two months, the business was " ordinary ", both branches, however, being subject to the principle of insurable interest. This doctrine had been part of the general law of life assurance for nearly 150 years, which had laid it down that no insurance could be taken out by a person on the life of another, or on an event, unless he had an interest therein, a husband or wife being presumed to have an insurable interest to any amount in the life of the spouse. In the industrial branch, however, relatives who might have to pay for funeral expenses had come, quite reasonably perhaps, to take it for granted that they could insure for this purpose, and the practice had grown up among the offices of permitting such insurances to be made. In strict law, of course, this might have been wrong: but the matter was put on a right footing by the major Act governing the business, the Assurance Companies Act, 1909, which authorised insurance for funeral expenses within certain relationships.

The Refuge was not affected by the section relating to the increased frequency of financial investigations, for the office had been making these and submitting them to the Board of Trade annually for some time past. Neither was the definition of the term " actuary ", which

75

at last received statutory status, a matter of any concern, for W. H. Aldcroft had been qualified for over fifteen years.   But it was certainly interested in the section empowering companies and collecting societies to issue policies covering the funeral expenses of a parent, grandparent, grandchild, brother or sister, and in particular validating all such existing policies taken out in good faith.   As was said in the debate on the Bill, the very existence of so many policies showed that they met a legitimate and proper need.

It is interesting to note that no limit was placed on the amount of funeral expenses to be assured.   This was done in practice by the offices themselves, who would only consider " reasonable " costs.   A very curious thing was the omission of " child " from the list of permitted relationships.   This is understood to have been due to a misunderstanding of the position, and in fact policies continued to be issued on the lives of children until the error was corrected in a later Act.

Closely following upon the passing of the 1909 Act, the company was called upon to consider the possible impact upon their business of another statute, Mr. Lloyd George's National Health Insurance Act of 1911.   Health insurance is, of course, quite different from industrial assurance, and in the absence of any provision for a death benefit the provisions of the Act would not have concerned the offices and their staffs.   Actually, however, they became involved at the direct request of Mr. Lloyd George who was well aware that his scheme would work the better if the Government would keep out of it.   It was Liberal tradition to avoid Government intervention in economic affairs unless absolutely necessary: and there were already in existence organisations which could take the administration of his scheme in their stride.   As he himself put it when introducing his Bill

" . . . These Societies are managed with great skill by men of consummate business ability, and the reason I say that is not because I want to buy off opposition but because I want their help. . . . We do not propose to interfere in the slightest degree with their present business. . . . But I do not rest there.   I should like to get the

JOHN HARRISON

MAIN ENTRANCE & CLOCK TOWER

The Tower, No. 2 Building

active aid and co-operation of these societies with their magnificent machinery. . . . So far from the collecting societies being injured, it would be a magnificent thing for them. But it would be a still better thing for the State to secure all this machinery for the purpose of working out this great scheme ".

The machinery, which was, of course, the weekly calls at millions of homes by agents of the offices, was in fact secured on a basis which was eminently reasonable and fair to all parties concerned. The scheme was administered by what were termed "approved societies" subject to certain guiding principles:—They must not be conducted for profit; they must be controlled by the majority vote of members; and the funds must be entirely distinct from the other funds of the sponsoring body. An individual assurance office could thus become, for national health insurance purposes, an approved society: and it was the original idea that the Refuge should set up its own approved society. Much of the preparatory work was in fact carried out and draft rules were prepared: subsequently, however, it was decided to join with a group of other offices in the association in the foundation of a joint body known as the National Amalgamated Approved Society.

As a result new duties were added to those already being carried out by the field staff. They now had the responsibility of conducting the national health insurance affairs of every person who chose to join the Refuge section of the National Amalgamated, which involved the distribution and subsequent collection of contribution cards, notification of claims, payment of benefits—all at the homes of the members, by the agents concerned. The office work was initiated at the district offices, passed on to a department at chief office created and staffed for this specific purpose, and then summarised and controlled by the head office of the National Amalgamated in London, in a fine building in Euston Square.

The Refuge was represented on the governing body of the society throughout its existence, which endured from its inception in 1912 to its being taken over by the Ministry of National Insurance consequent on the passing of the National Insurance Act in 1946. The full list is as follows:

Date of Appointment	Name	Position	Subsequent
1912	R. W. GREEN	Vice-President	1915 President
	PHILIP SMITH	Joint Treasurer	
	WM. EDWARDS	Committee	1918 Trustee
	JAS. S. PROCTOR	Committee	1920 Vice-Chairman
			1922 Vice-President
			1925 President
1916	W. H. ALDCROFT, F.I.A.	Consulting Actuary	
1922	J. PROCTOR GREEN	Committee	1932 Joint Treasurer
1925	J. WILCOCK HOLGATE	Joint Treasurer	1928 Vice-Chairman
			1936 Chairman
1928	F. W. D. MOTTERSHEAD, F.F.I.	Committee	
1944	WM. PROCTOR SMITH	Joint Treasurer	1946 Treasurer

In the first quarter of 1912, the Refuge had 474,150 members out of a total in the society of 1,585,536.

The scheme was conducted on an actuarial basis, which involved valuations every five years. Any surplus disclosed could only be distributed as the Government Valuer might approve, and only by way of increased benefits to the members. It was, therefore, the earnest endeavour of every approved society, not merely to hold its own as regards benefits, but so to work as to increase them: there was keen competition among them; and this was no doubt an important factor in securing the satisfactory surpluses that emerged at successive valuations. In view of what has occurred following the taking over in

1948 of the approved societies it is interesting—and perhaps instructive —to read the following extract from the Summary Report of the Government Actuary on the Fifth Valuation of the Assets and Liabilities of Approved Societies, dated April 22nd, 1943.

TABLE V

Analysis of Surplus Resources at the Fourth and Fifth Valuations and their disposal.

		Fourth Valuation £ millions	Fifth Valuation £ millions
Aggregate Surpluses		37.5	34.3
add: estimated savings from schemes of treatment additional benefits current at the valuation date		2.8	3.7
		40.3	38.0
Deduct: estimated amount applied to additional benefits after valuation		21.6	20.5
Balance carried forward		18.7	17.5
Contingencies Funds	3.3		3.6
Add: Grants from Central Fund ..	0.5		0.6
	3.8		4.2
Deduct: aggregate deficiencies ..	0.8		0.9
Balance of Contingencies Funds not required to meet deficiencies		3.0	3.3
Total sum carried forward after valuation		21.7	20.8

Truly the industrial assurance organisations would appear to have deserved well of the country.

Prior to 1912, the accounts of the company had been audited by persons possessing no professional qualifications: and it was now thought proper that the duty should be entrusted to qualified accountants. A resolution to this effect was passed at an ordinary general meeting, on March 4th, 1912, and the choice fell upon Tom and Henry Bailey Walton, of the firm of Walton, Watts and Co., chartered accountants, of Manchester: and this firm has been responsible for the auditors' report to the shareholders continuously from that date.

In the same year the death occurred of the chairman, James Wilcock. He had been connected with the company for 44 years, being appointed a director in 1884 and chairman in 1898. He was succeeded by R. W. Green.

Prior to 1913 the company had relied for legal advice on a succession of solicitors who acted for it in a consultative capacity. The first member of its own staff to qualify as a solicitor was John W. Proctor, in 1899, and he was formally appointed solicitor to the company in 1906. It is extremely unlikely that he actually functioned as such, since he was already a director and joint general manager. The first " employed resident solicitor " was John Harrison, who was appointed in 1913. He had left school when he was 12 or 14 years of age, and in his early days his intention had been to study chemistry, being at one time employed by a Manchester firm of wholesale chemists. He joined the office in 1899, and in 1908, when he was 34 years of age, he was articled to William P. Green, one of the company's unattached solicitors. He served five years' articles, and studied in his spare time, being admitted a solicitor in 1913. His examination record was brilliant, winning the John Mackrell and New Inn prizes and obtaining first-class honours in the honours examination held in 1913. Fundamentally sound, he was a very able lawyer, and as a practical man a most valuable official in a wide variety of ways. He was not only highly regarded by the management and board of the Refuge but was also held in very high esteem in the Industrial Life Offices Association in London. He served on the legal sub-committee of the association for over 20 years, and gave evidence before the Cohen Committee prior to its report in 1933. He retired in 1946, but was retained as consultant until his death in 1955, at the age of 81. He was succeeded by his nephew, Cyril C. Harrison, who is at present the company's solicitor.

Barely ten years after the company had moved to its new offices in Oxford Street, it was becoming abundantly clear that the accommodation provided was quite insufficient to house the staff, documents and records required to administer the ever-increasing flood of business: and on April 17th, 1905, it was resolved that the offices be enlarged by building an extension on the Oxford Street site. The architect appointed was Paul Waterhouse, M.A., the son of Waterhouse who designed No. 1 building. The site was rather an awkward one, being roughly triangular in shape, owing to the course of the River Medlock, which runs underneath Oxford Street at this point and borders the new building in a slanting direction. Externally, it completed the original design facing Oxford Street, the whole comprising a distinctly impressive edifice: internally, however, it was never quite the success of its predecessor in a functional sense. It was certainly more elaborate, containing a remarkably handsome marble staircase which ran from top to bottom, from attic to basement, with elaborately designed bronze handrails and lamp-brackets. For many years this show piece —for that indeed it was—was forbidden territory to the staff, some of the retired members of whom still remember the day when a daring office boy, using it as a short cut, was so very unfortunate as to drop a bottle of ink on it. According to legend, it was a very sad affair altogether.

It was at this stage that the tower was erected, forming a most impressive addition to the Manchester sky-line, especially from the open area to the south. From street level to the top of the cupola it is 217 feet high and contains a clock, with four faces, from which thousands of Manchester citizens nowadays take their time. The five minute intervals are indicated on each face by glass bees— the original device of the office: the quarters with open, the remainder with closed, wings. The minute hand is 7 feet 10 inches long and weighs 60 lb. The clock used to be wound by hand, the underlying depth of the tower being just sufficient to accept the driving weight at its lowest point. It is to-day driven off batteries, with provision for transfer to the mains if required. The principal entrance to the office is through archways at the base of the tower, guarded by a beautiful set of wrought-iron gates, within which is a courtyard which now houses the Memorial to those of the staff who died in two Great Wars.

The accommodation provided was about the same as in No. 1 building; and it had the advantage of electric light from the outset— very different from its predecessor, from which the gas fittings were only then in process of being removed. The system then was the incandescent upright and fork, and it was the task of four men to go round the place with tapers when darkness fell—rather like interior lamp-lighters. Electricity was not installed until 1908: an impressive thought in view of the striking changes that have taken place since then. There are, after all, only 55 years between the horse-tram and Zeta.

The new offices were not opened any too soon, for No. 1 building had become as congested as had been the old premises in Corporation Street. The fact was that the company had weathered its early storms, had completed its organisation, had equipped itself with an efficient field staff—from whom, after all, the new business must flow— and was reaping an ample harvest from the general prosperity that characterised the opening years of the present century. Industrial assurance now had the cachet, so to speak, of the Acts of 1870 and 1909 to give it standing in the public mind: and there is no doubt that Mr. Lloyd George was right in saying that in helping the Government to administer national health insurance the offices could have no better advertisement of their own worth and integrity. Certainly, the progress of the Refuge, by the standard of new policies issued, was remarkable: in 1913 the figures were:

		No. of Policies effected	Total sums assured
Ordinary branch	..	56,151	£3,353,006
Industrial branch	..	1,313,869	£14,728,240

Work and War

RAPID EXPANSION: J. G. MARRIOTT: THE FIRST GREAT WAR, 1914—1918

THE figures set out at the end of the previous chapter were the fruits of a policy of expansion followed by the company over a period of several years, and latterly most successfully developed by an outstanding field man named J. G. Marriott. When first promoted from superintendent he was appointed inspector to the Sheffield area where he made rapid progress. He was then sent to Newcastle-upon-Tyne as branch manager and later to Scotland, where he repeated his success. In 1913 he was brought to chief office in the newly-created position of general inspector in control of the whole of the company's operations in the field excepting in London, Manchester and Blackburn. By this time the process had been completed of dividing the whole of the country into different inspectorates.

Simultaneously with the creation of these inspectorates, styled divisions, the organisation within chief office was modified to fit in with the new idea, and the whole office was divided into groups each dealing with every aspect of the business of one, two or three divisions, each managed in identical fashion, and each corresponding directly with its outside officials.

About this time the coal miners came out on strike for a minimum wage of 5s. per day; and the idea of a minimum wage was adopted by the Refuge for its agents, at the rate of 25s. per week for married men and 20s. per week for the single, plus, of course, commission on new business and the usual first year and renewal commissions in the ordinary branch. The results were unfortunate. Taken in con-

R. W. GREEN, J.P.

Volunteers from Chief Office, August, 1914

1. G. Cryer	16. K. Stevenson	30. F. Burgess	44. S. Brookes
2. G. Moss	17. J. Strong	31. A. Forrest	45. F. Morton
3. T. Winter (Com.)	18. J. A. Moore	32. H. Fenton	46. J. Penn
4. J. Wood	19. H. Hawxby	33. E. Harrison	47. R. Burrows
5. H. Toft	20. H. W. Platford	34. E. Gooch	48. F. Webster
6. H. F. Davis	21. J. Byrne	35. J. A. Bingham	49. W. Caldwell
7. W. Wickman	22. C. Stuttard	36. S. Windsor	50. R. W. Green
8. N. Feay	23. F. Lockwood	37. M. Richardson	51. F. Hibbert.
9. H. Smith	24. T. Yarwood	38. W. Greaves	52. J. Catterall
10. G. Hatton	25. C. Horobin	39. J. Scott	53. T. Upton
11. W. Jackson	26. H. Isherwood	40. H. Baguley	54. A. Sewell
12. P. Darlington	27. A. Stuttard	41. H. P. Wright	55. A. Shepherd
13. F. Warren	28. G. Ashmore	42. J. Ellis	56. W. Hartland
14. H. Smith	29. D. Murphy	43. W. Turner	57. J. Bowker
15. W. Stenson			

junction with a rapid increase in the number of districts, which had averaged 400 (1895—1900), 500 (1900—1905), 700 (1905—1910), reaching a peak of nearly 900 about 1914, the expenses, albeit expenses of expansion, became uneconomic. The new districts were in the main small as to debit value and it became clear that it was essential to have larger administrative units. As a result, a process of contraction in the number of districts was carefully and deliberately instigated.

It was fortunate that this policy had already been adopted when the first Great War broke out in August, 1914. The company was at once faced with two major problems relating respectively to staff and to policyholders. Another serious problem, not immediately apparent, was to be the future gradual increase in costs of all descriptions consequent on war conditions.

As regards the staff, all reservists and Territorials were called up at once; and almost simultaneously there was a rush to volunteer for service in the Forces. To fill the vacancies in the field recourse was had to retired men, pensioners, men unfit for service and, in particular, women. It was not a new thing to appoint a woman agent—it will be remembered that almost fifty years before, Selina Leader had served as a collector for the original society. But now things were different: the men simply were not there to employ, and so we see wives, daughters, fiancées of Refuge field men filling their places, together with other women who also played their part in releasing the menfolk for their newly arrived preoccupation. It is to be recorded that these temporary recruits to the field force fulfilled their novel task magnificently, quite a number of them revealing quite unsuspected talents for the business.

At chief office tradition was blown to the winds; and not only did the company engage large numbers of women, chiefly young girls, but it spread them all over the office. It was interesting to observe how naturally they fell into place, and how well they worked with their male colleagues—who became sadly fewer and fewer as the war went on.

The question of the existing policyholders was most serious, for the problem was one of entirely unknown proportions. The board most certainly did not subscribe to the " all over by Christmas " illusion. Equally, however, not a single member could foresee that the conflict was to continue over four years, and to assume a more deadly character with each week that went by. Nevertheless, from the very early disastrous days it was apparent that casualties were going to be very high.

All the Refuge policies in the ordinary branch included a war clause, i.e., they excluded deaths amongst members of the Armed Forces as a result of war. If the company were to stand on the clause, it would discourage recruiting and cause added distress to the relatives of those who might lose their lives. On the other hand to suspend it might have serious, even disastrous effects on the financial resources of the office. It is good to recall that within the Refuge, as within the whole of the industry, there was no hesitation: the clause was suspended for all existing policies, with only the saving qualification that the doing so did not make it contractual, and that it might be re-imposed should such a step become actually necessary. On this score the different boards must have had many heart-searchings as the claims rose higher and higher: but they never changed their minds, and the clause remained suspended until the war was over.

A quite unexpected step was taken by the Government in the passing of the Courts (Emergency Powers) Act, 1914, which enacted that life assurances effected before August 4th, 1912, for sums not exceeding £25 could not be treated as lapsed by non-payment of premiums without the authority of the court. The fear, of course, was that the war would cause widespread poverty and distress; but in fact the economic status of the industrial branch policyholders rose appreciably, and in the event there was little need for a statute directly opposed to the elementary principle of life assurance. It caused a further strain on the company's resources by making it liable to pay claims on large numbers of policies protected against forfeiture by non-payment of premiums; and that liability was continued for some years after the end of the war. At one time the total premiums so unpaid amounted to over £500,000, and the item did not disappear from the balance sheet until 1927.

It remained to be decided what was to be done regarding financial help to those who had joined the fighting services and to their families. It was resolved to pay allowances on varying scales dependent on the differing circumstances, whether clerk, agent, official, single, married, etc., and these allowances were continued whatever advancements and consequent increases in pay were secured in a man's army career.

Week by week: almost day by day: the office was informed of men enlisting in the forces. It is a remarkable fact that for over two years Great Britain fought the war on the basis of voluntary enlistment: conscription did not come into force until May, 1916, and by that time the flower of a young generation had been destroyed. There was a moving scene at chief office in August, 1914, when nearly 60 clerks fell in in the courtyard at chief office and marched in formation to the depôt in Ardwick of the Manchester Regiment, where a series of Pals Battalions was being formed, in one of which they desired to enlist in a body. There were so many other volunteers at the time that this was not possible; but later on about half the number achieved their desire and served together until the battalions were decimated on July 16th, 1916, at Trônes Wood.

The staffing difficulties were greatly increased when conscription came in and stark necessity resulted in older and less fit men being accepted in the armed forces. Towards the end there came to be some truth as well as typical mordant humour in the Army description of a medical examination—" If you're warm—you're in ! " The gaps in the field and chief office ranks were filled more and more often by women and girls; and indeed there was a period of over ten years from 1914 to 1924 when hardly more than a handful of boys was recruited to the chief office staff—a circumstance known for years as " the gap " and which so affected the age distribution of the male employees as to create unlooked-for difficulties in later years.

Not the least of the company's contributions to the war effort was its loyal support of the Government loans throughout the whole period. At the close of the war, the chairman was able to report that the Refuge had participated in national war loans to the extent of over £6,191,000, representing $37\frac{1}{2}$ per cent. of the total invested funds.

The office could do little to avoid increases in its claim ratios, which were affected seriously by its determination to meet all war claims in full; while as regards expenses, it was desperately difficult to avoid increases in the ratios due to the ever-increasing costs of material of all kinds, the allowances to enlisted members of the staff, and the higher costs of inexperienced labour. The company had, in fact, to make the best of a situation which involved war-time cost of production with pre-war selling prices as regards the commodity in which it dealt, a situation with which no trading concern outside life assurance was required to cope.

Towards the end of the war, the company had to face a further financial strain in the influenza epidemic of 1918–19, which not only ravaged the Continent but swept this country from end to end, encouraged in its deadly work by war-time conditions—overcrowding, malnutrition, worry and the like. In 1918 alone death claims from this cause cost the company over £207,000: and the final figures were over £300,000 in addition to a total of nearly £900,000 in respect of war claims. The war allowances paid amounted to over £224,000.

The number of employees who served in the Forces was 3,089; and of these 285 gave their lives. The memorial in the courtyard stands today in their memory.

After that never-to-be-forgotten day of November 11th, 1918, the industrial position became one of considerable confusion. Plans for the demobilisation of members of the forces had long been prepared by the Government, and were put into force immediately: but the natural desire of the men to get home as soon as possible and to make sure of their civilian employment gave rise to considerable difficulty, there being no statutory obligation on employers to re-employ men returning from the Forces. Refuge men were in a happier position, the company having given a promise of reinstatement on return to civilian life: but for some time to come the consequent plethora of labour was something of an embarrassment.

It was a strange world indeed to which the men returned. Chief office was discovered to be in the occupation of women and girls, some of them carrying out quite senior work. Moreover, a staff of 806 males and 195 females in 1914 had become transformed into one of 324 males and 503 females by June 1st, 1919. The work, too, was not the same: not only were there changes in detail, which were to be expected and need worry no one, but in some respects in principle also, which certainly needed getting used to.

The field staff were to find things even more novel and difficult to adapt themselves to. The 839 districts of 1914 had diminished to 597 at the end of 1918. The full-time agency force, which in 1914 had consisted of nearly 6,000 men, had undergone a transformation, both in numbers and constitution, and at the end of 1918 was represented by 2,545 men and 1,330 women. Most important of all were the changes in the organisation of the field force and in their work, whereby the expansive schemes of 1913 had been modified to the more closely-knit arrangements rendered necessary by war conditions, and proved to be more effective and economic in their own right.

The company was naturally sympathetic to those of their temporary staffs who had proved their worth and done so much to enable the office to maintain its full services to policyholders and the country during four most difficult years; and every effort was made to consider their interests so far as was compatible with those of the returning men. As events turned out, it was found possible at chief office to retain on the staff the greater portion of those who wished to remain: whilst in the field, most of the temporary staff were happy to return home, having made a very fine job of holding the fort until the proper holders returned to their civilian posts.

CHAPTER X

Reorganisation

RECONSTRUCTION: BLOCKING OF DEBITS: GENERAL INSPECTORS:
GENERAL INSURANCE: FORMATION OF STAFF ASSOCIATIONS:
PENSION SCHEME: INDUSTRIAL ASSURANCE ACT, 1923.

DURING the war it had not been possible to pursue the company's
policy of gradual reduction in the rate of expense. Having regard to
the heavy charges due to the times, as for example the allowances to
serving men, the comparative expensiveness of inexperienced and
temporary staff, the increased costs of all materials, etc., it was as much
as could be done merely to avoid actual increases in the rate, and this
was in fact achieved. As soon, however, as post-war conditions permitted, the policy of economy was renewed. "Blocking" enabled
agents to conduct larger debits; business was concentrated into fewer
districts; and the number of inspectorates was reduced. This was
rendered possible by the much improved means of communication
then available. It was only fifteen years since the last horse tram
clanked through the streets of Manchester; but in 1918 there were not
only electric trams, but petrol buses had made their appearance. It
was the beginning of the petrol age, and all the ampler means of movement it was to provide.

Immediately prior to the war, the company had had under consideration a major alteration in its agency organisation in the industrial
branch. Up to this time an agent had been free to wander at will to
secure new business and subsequently to collect the weekly or monthly
premium. This meant that in any given area there would be over-
lapping as between agents, with all that that implied in waste of time
and effort: and the answer seemed to be to divide definite areas into

91

what could be called " blocks ", varying in size according to the density of the population, within which one agent only would represent the office. By thus concentrating his debit, an agent would be saved both time and money previously expended in travelling, and it would be possible to increase his debit and consequently his earnings.

The process of blocking, wherever possible, was begun in June, 1915, and within a year 50 per cent. of the agencies had come within the scope of these arrangements. Two years after the end of the war the scheme was virtually complete, the average debit per agent being increased by nearly fifty per cent., and the number of districts having decreased by one third. A good beginning had thus been made in the programme of concentration, which has been carried out systematically from that day to this; whereby despite increases in the earnings of the staff over-all economies have been secured.

At chief office also, reorganisation was the order of the day. Machinery was beginning to appear in a variety of forms; and this means of labour saving was adopted wherever it was practicable. Typewriters appeared in profusion, with especially beneficial effects in the policy-writing department. Calculating machines ceased to be the proud possession of the privileged few and—most significantly—a punched card system was introduced in the actuarial department whereby card preparation, sorting and tabulation could be carried out mechanically in much less time and involving many fewer clerks than had formerly been necessary when the work was done by hand. The system was to grow impressively as the years went on.

Whereas in pre-1914 days, women had only been engaged on policy-writing or copying work in a separate department, the experience of the war years had shown how suitable for girls was much of the routine work all over the office. Since it was very difficult in the immediate post-war years to attract to the business boys of the right type, recourse was had to a steady influx of young girls to fill the vacancies arising through deaths, retirements or—in the case of the

W. H. Aldcroft, F.I.A.

J. G. Marriott   T. R. Mitchell   Jabez Pearson

W. Edwards   Albert Swift

General Inspectors, 1919

women—marriages. The tightening up of the organisation in the field had an immediate effect upon the demand for labour at chief office; and the outcome was to reduce the clerical staff to 426 males and 388 females in 1921. Since that date the proportion of females has further increased and now represents two-thirds of the total clerical grades.

It has already been recorded that J. G. Marriott, in 1913, had been appointed general inspector for the company: and in 1919 it was resolved to create four more similar appointments to assist him in his work and particularly in the task of reorganisation. The men selected, and the areas allotted to them, were as follows:

T. R. MITCHELL .. (Blackburn)
WM. EDWARDS .. (London and the south)
J. PEARSON .. (Liverpool, Wales, Birmingham, Potteries, Carlisle)
A. SWIFT .. (Manchester, Warrington, Bolton, Scotland)

The remaining area, the north-east, was to remain in the care of J. G. Marriott.

T. R. Mitchell was appointed to the Blackburn office in 1879, and was connected with that area throughout his career. Blackburn was one of the original director-areas. Situated as it was in the heart of the prosperous cotton and manufacturing area of Lancashire, it became a very important part of the company's organisation. It came to serve as a subsidiary chief office in south-east Lancashire and had a large office staff carrying out, on behalf of chief office, many of the clerical and administrative duties associated with the operations of the large number of districts in the division. T. R. Mitchell had passed through all the clerical grades in this important office, eventually becoming inspector in charge of the area. He served as general inspector from 1919 until his retirement in 1923.

William Edwards began his career as a clerk in the Livesey Street

Office in 1879. He later became an agent in the Hulme district, then assistant at Salford, and subsequently superintendent at Weaste. He was appointed inspector at the London City office in 1901, and as branch manager was put in control of Division II, a wide area south of London, in 1914. He served as general inspector from 1919 to 1925, when he retired. He continued his active connection in an official capacity with the National Amalgamated Approved Society until it was taken over by the Ministry of Health, in 1948. He was awarded the M.B.E., and for many years acted as a local preacher, a practice which he kept up until his death in 1956, at the age of 91.

Jabez Pearson was a field man throughout his career. He joined the company in 1888 as an agent at Blackburn. He became an assistant at Otley in 1892 and later served as superintendent in five different districts over a period of five years. He was appointed inspector at Blackburn in 1901, was transferred to the Liverpool division in 1905, and served as general inspector from 1919 until his death in 1923.

Albert Swift had a very long and varied career, occupying in turn every field position outside chief office. He began as an agent in 1890, and became successively assistant (1897), superintendent (1904), assistant inspector (1905), inspector (1910), general inspector (1919) and finally, agency manager in chief office in 1930, a position he held until his retirement in 1938.

An interesting minute appears in the report of the board meeting on March 29th, 1920, to the effect that J. Wilcock Holgate suggested that the company should undertake general branch business. The idea was mooted again the following August, and the next month, after a lengthy discussion, the joint general manager, W. H. Aldcroft, was instructed to get out particulars as to the workings of a general branch. It was an unfortunate time to consider such a striking development. The brief post-war boom was nearly over, and the signs of depression were only too evident; whilst the newly-returned and reorganised staff, both at chief office and in the field, were not yet ready to add new and intricate forms of insurance to their existing pre-occupations with life assurance. It seems to have been decided to put the scheme on one side for the time being; and although it was dis-cussed again from time to time, no definite steps were taken until 1953, when the company purchased the shares of the Federated Employers' Insurance Association, Ltd., through which a growing amount of general business is now administered on behalf of the Refuge.

Among the many post-war problems confronting the company was unrest among the staffs. This was not a phenomenon confined solely to the Refuge: it applied to industries all over the country, and was a natural reaction from years of service and experience in an unpleasant and singularly dangerous war. The men returning felt that they deserved—and indeed they had been promised—a world fit for heroes to live in. It could not help but be an anticlimax to come back to civilian pursuits—safe, certainly, but not exciting; at wages which they soon found had not kept up with the cost of living. The brief post-war period of boom and consequent inflation was under way, and it was a natural desire to share in the prosperity which apparently abounded. It was a period of Whitley Councils and Trade Boards.

The company took a sympathetic view towards this ambition so far as their own staff at chief office was concerned; and a general increase in salaries was prepared and came into force in October, 1919. It was also proposed by the management that a staff council should be set up:—To elect its own officers; with leave to meet on office premises and in office time; and to meet representatives of the management from time to time, with the purpose of ensuring close contact between staff and company. The proposal was accepted by the staff committee then in being, subject to the management recognising their right to consult, and in case of deadlock bring into discussion, the Guild of Insurance Officials, of which the committee was already a branch. The first meeting of the staff council took place on June 14th, 1920; and since

95

then half-yearly and special interviews have been held with the management, at which free and comprehensive expressions of views have been exchanged and to which the Guild has been called only in cases of deadlock over new scales of remuneration. The arrangement has worked to good effect over the years, principally because both sides are enabled to hear and to appreciate the other's point of view. This understanding, and a willingness to accept facts, are the basis of good staff relations; and the inauguration of the staff council appears thoroughly to have justified itself.

The first honorary secretary was a well-known figure at chief office, named Lawrence Ashmore, M.Comm., who was more or less pitch-forked into this post on the joint strength of his reputation and his degree, which he had obtained in 1915 by spare-time study at Manchester University. He was an excellent choice, and his minutes are models of clarity. He later became a divisional head (1925), industrial branch controller (1933), and finally, joint general manager in 1946. He had an encyclopædic knowledge of the staff, both at chief office and in the field. Small in stature, and a shade rotund, his appearance and his inscrutable countenance when about to say " No " justified his affectionate nickname of " the little Buddha ".

Amongst the field force, too, a similar situation developed; and, also in 1919, the management was in agreement with the suggestion that a field staff association be created, with which the company could deal as representing the whole of the outside staff. Prior to this date there had been an association of Refuge field men in South Wales, with a dynamic personality named Edgar Jones as secretary, then an assistant superintendent for the company. When the proposal of the company to form a country-wide association was put forward, it was obvious that the work involved in being secretary would be far too great for any man to regard as a spare-time occupation: whilst moreover, it would clearly be necessary to find a headquarters and a staff. Most important of all, however, was the desire amongst the staff that the proposed association should be an independent body, registered as a trade union. The company does not appear to have regarded these desires as unreasonable: for not only did the management agree to release Edgar Jones to be the first general secretary, but they agreed also to re-employ him if he so desired if for any reason he relinquished his new office. It was clearly not practicable—and certainly undesirable—for an independent staff body to occupy any part of chief office; and although every facility was offered in the formative weeks of the association by the provision of accommodation, clerical assistance, stationery, etc., it was accepted that separate headquarters should be established elsewhere, and this was done in Levenshulme, Manchester, in 1921.

The association was to be made up of four separate grades: superintendents, assistants, agents and clerks. Each grade was to have its separate executive to deal with matters peculiar to itself, and from the whole a national executive was to be elected, to negotiate on any matter on a national basis. The general secretary was to be a full-time salaried employee of the association; whilst the president for the time being was to be elected from among the full-time employees of the company. Interviews at regular intervals were to be held with the management; and it was agreed that the officials of the association would be allowed facilities to carry out the duties of their respective positions.

The company having agreed upon the constitution and method of operation of the proposed association, it fell to the lot of Edgar Jones to establish branches all over the country and to build up the membership. He accomplished this most successfully, increasing the original 70 to 5,000. He remained in office until 1926 when his health failed him, and once more he found employment with the company, finally retiring in 1936.

In the interviews between the association and the company, complete freedom of expression is the rule. The personal contact is of particular value since field men so seldom have the opportunity of visiting chief office and sensing, as it were, the atmosphere of management *vis-à-vis* the outside men.

Simultaneously with the setting up of the two staff associations, the company announced details of the new pension arrangements it had been decided to make. For many years pensions had been granted to retiring employees, but not according to any fixed scales, and payable only at the discretion of the company. It was felt that the time had come to regularise the practice and so definite rules were laid down as to qualifying period of service, age of retirement, proportion of earnings or salary to be paid as pension, and joint life options in the case of married men. A scale of gratuities payable on the death of active members of the staff was also issued. The pensions, once granted, were no longer to be continued at the " will and pleasure " of the company, but became a right conferred upon the recipient. The setting up of the scheme was a forward-looking action on the part of the company and was naturally warmly received by the entire staff, the more so as it was entirely non-contributory on their part and so constituted a significant addition to the value of their remuneration.

Industrial assurance, as a business, has several times been the subject of committees of inquiry over the last hundred years—reasonably enough perhaps, in view of the very large sums that came to be involved, and the fact that the offices were in the position of trustees towards millions of individuals of small means who had entrusted to them their provision for the future, whether in respect of old age or death. One such inquiry was set on foot in 1919 under the chairmanship of Lord Parmoor with a view to ascertaining whether any amendment of the law was desirable. The report of the committee was issued in 1920, and contained a number of recommendations, with some of which the offices, on reasoned grounds, could not agree. The sequel was a draft Bill introduced into the House of Lords on August 10th, 1921, by Lord Onslow, in the words: " In moving the second reading of this Bill I should like again to express the hope that it may receive the consideration and criticism of those who are interested therein between now and next session, so that when the Government introduce the Bill again they may be in possession of the view of those who are interested in this subject." The opportunity thus so sensibly afforded was fully utilised, all parties concerned being able to make their views and arguments generally known: and these discussions were to lead up to the passing of the Industrial Assurance Act, 1923, which was henceforth to exercise an over-riding control over the business.

In the preliminary negotiations the lead for the industry was taken by the Association of Industrial Assurance Companies and Collecting Friendly Societies, the staff organisations, and the Prudential Assurance Company. On the recommendation of the Home Secretary, a small committee was appointed and something like agreement was reached with the Government. The company was represented on the committee by J. Proctor Green, and the staff by G. A. Jarvis and Edgar Jones (Refuge Field Staff Association) and officers of the Guild of Insurance Officials, acting for—amongst others—the Refuge Staff Council. The company's assistant actuary, S. G. Leigh, had already served on a committee of actuaries set up by the offices to meet frequently in London during the sittings of the Parmoor Committee. This committee remained in being in an advisory capacity throughout the discussions which preceded the passing of the Act. Separate points were agreed upon as follows: The making of a substantial deposit; separation of the industrial assurance fund; freedom of administration; adequate reserves; checks on " transferring "; rules regarding the amalgamation of offices; and protection of the interests of policyholders who could no longer maintain their premium payments. Provisions covering these points were embodied in the Act, together with a number of others which, *in toto*, made up an instrument of control which has since functioned with complete success in the interests of all parties concerned—the Government, the policyholders and the offices.

Perhaps the most important provision was the creation of the office of Industrial Assurance Commissioner, charged with the duty of seeing that all the provisions of the Act were duly carried out, and for this purpose being invested with very wide powers; whilst reserving to the offices complete freedom in conducting their affairs within the framework thus laid down. The immediate effect upon the Refuge as one of the offices concerned was: (a) to require the deposit of £20,000 in respect of the industrial branch just as had been required by the Act of 1909 in respect of the ordinary branch; (b) properly to apportion between the two branches all expenses of management; (c) to render to the Commissioner revenue accounts, balance sheets, and actuarial valuations on appropriate bases as was already being done with the Board of Trade; (d) to instruct the field staff fully as to their new duties as regards proposals, policies, premium receipt-books and notices of forfeiture; and (e) to ensure that free policy and cash surrender values were properly calculated and duly granted.

Two other provisions were of major importance. The Courts (Emergency Powers) Act, 1914, ceased to be in force; and it was made clear that policies insuring money to be paid for the funeral expenses of a child were permissible.

One section of the Act dealing with the case of a policyholder who might allow a policy to lapse and then take out another in its place, had a curious result. In order to avoid the difficulties consequent on a later ruling by the Commissioner's office as to what precisely a " substituted " policy was, the Refuge, in common with many other offices, set up a system of automatic free policies, whereby any policyholder who had paid not less than two years' premiums on an assurance which he allowed to lapse was granted a free policy for a reduced amount. This is now effected by the issue of a memorandum: but at the beginning the lapsed policy was endorsed with a statement of free policy and returned to the policyholder, often enough to his considerable surprise. It is worth recalling the case of a gentleman, by profession a

War Memorial
(*an Artist's Impression*)

Diamond Jubilee, Free Trade Hall, Manchester

bookmaker, who allowed a policy to lapse, and in due course had it returned to him duly endorsed as a free policy for a smaller amount. He immediately returned it to the company with a note scrawled across it to this effect: " Keep it. When I back a horse that doesn't stay the course, I don't ask for my money back."

The actuarial department still treasure his memory.

CHAPTER XI

Between the Wars

POST-WAR DEPRESSION: DEATH OF R. W. GREEN: WAR
MEMORIAL: DIAMOND JUBILEE: DEATH OF PHILIP SMITH: THE
GENERAL STRIKE: HOUSE PURCHASE BUSINESS: MANCHESTER
CIVIC WEEK: DEATH OF JAS. S. PROCTOR: ALLOCATION OF
PROFITS TO INDUSTRIAL BRANCH POLICYHOLDERS: NEW
APPOINTMENTS AT CHIEF OFFICE: WORLD-WIDE FINANCIAL
CRISES: EXPENSE RATIOS AND VALUATION BASES: COHEN
INQUIRY: OPENING OF NO. 3 BUILDING: SUPERANNUATION
TRUST FUND: TRANSFER OF EIRE BUSINESS.

IT has already been remarked that industrial conditions just after
the war were quite abnormal, not only in this country but in the world
generally. They continued so for over ten years. There seem to have
been three distinct stages:—At first, following the general upset caused
by demobilisation, there were two years of boom conditions, when high
hopes were held of general recovery: then followed three years of
severe depression: succeeded by a gradual improvement ending
suddenly about 1930 in a world-wide economic blizzard. These were
the conditions the company and its staff were called upon to face—and
to overcome.

The immediate effect on the company of the industrial depression
which continued from 1921 to 1924 was an increasing difficulty in
securing the due payment of premiums. It was, and still is, traditional
in the business to allow a generous number of weeks' premiums to be in
arrears before notices of forfeiture are issued: but in the circumstances
then prevailing even the maximum limit of 13 weeks proved insufficient. It was necessary to adopt exceptional methods and the board
thereupon resolved, in cases of proved hardship, temporarily to forgo

the payment of premiums, allowing them to remain a debt upon the policies, or, in cases where several policies were involved, to allow one or more to be surrendered for cash upon generous terms in order to keep the remainder in force. These measures were applied particularly to the coal mining districts and to what were known as the "depressed areas"—areas in which cotton, iron, or shipping were the principal occupations. When at last conditions began to improve, the arrears were gradually extinguished over a very long period; and it is a tribute both to the persistence of the staffs, and to the value placed by the holders upon their policies, that so many contracts eventually emerged intact from the turmoil of strikes, lock-outs, and plain unemployment.

In 1922 the death occurred of R. W. Green, the chairman of the company. He had been a director since 1890; and had served as joint general manager from 1898 until 1912, when he was elected chairman of the board. He had been a member of the executive of the Industrial Life Offices Association—as the old association is now known—since its formation: and had been president of the National Amalgamated Approved Society for several years prior to his death. He was for many years a Justice of the Peace for Cheshire. He was succeeded as chairman by James S. Proctor.

Very soon after the end of the war, the board took steps to collate all the relevant information to enable them to prepare a suitable record of those Refuge men who had served in the forces, and in particular, to erect within the office precincts a memorial "not only to those who made the supreme sacrifice, but also to that greater number who endured the hardships and perils of the ordeal and who were spared to return".

The site chosen was the centre of the courtyard. The memorial itself was executed in grey Cornish granite, standing 26 feet high on a square base, with rounded angles. It is crowned by a figure of Victory, five feet in height, holding a laurel wreath and palm branch.

Three of the four sides bear cast bronze panels on which appear the names of the fallen. The front panel bears the dedication inscription, which reads:

IN HONOUR OF THOSE OF THE STAFF OF THE REFUGE ASSURANCE COMPANY, LTD., WHO SERVED IN THE WAR 1914–1918 AND IN LOVING MEMORY OF THOSE WHO FELL.

" Let those who come after see to it
that their names be not forgotten."

The unveiling ceremony took place on November 28th, 1922, attended by relatives of the fallen as guests of the company, and representatives of the board, management, and all grades of the staff. It fell to the new chairman, Jas. S. Proctor, to unveil this tribute to so many of the company's employees; and the service was conducted by the Archdeacon of Manchester, the Venerable Noel Lake Aspinall, M.A.

Ever since that day, each year on November 11th, wreaths are laid on the plinth by representatives of the board, management, staff associations, and the ex-servicemen's association.

In 1924, it was decided to celebrate in some fitting fashion the completion of the sixtieth year of the existence of the Refuge as a company. In the case of the field staff, divisional staff luncheons were held throughout the country, to be attended by one or other of the general managers. In the case of the chief office staff, the company acted as host on the occasion of the then annual picnic which on this occasion was held at Windermere, towards the end of June.

Finally, a giant luncheon and conference was arranged, to be attended by the board and management, and by as many members of the staff as could be accommodated. The affair now remains a fragment of Manchester history: for it involved the famous Free Trade Hall and the well-known Midland Hotel in a fashion which was unique at the time and has remained so ever since—and will indeed remain for ever, for the old Free Trade Hall is now no more. It was destroyed by bombs in 1940, and was rebuilt in very different form: the accompanying photograph will arouse nostalgic memories in the minds of those people who used to know it so well.

The guests at the luncheon and tea numbered 902; and the arrangements for the meals were entrusted to the Midland Hotel, who were thus made responsible not only for the transformation of what was normally a concert hall into a banqueting room, but also for the even greater task of transferring from the hotel to the hall two entire kitchens, together with the complete equipment for the service of two meals to nearly a thousand people—carpets, tables, chairs, napery, crockery, plate, glass, decoration, etc. It is worthy of record that the hotel, of necessity, had only eleven hours in which to effect the change, and that the work was completed with fifteen minutes to spare.

It is interesting to compare the present day preference for few and short speeches with the practice of the past. In those days speeches tended to be many and lengthy: but even so, the conference in the afternoon seems to have been over-supplied with speakers. They numbered 33!

The year witnessed the issuing of the millionth policy in the ordinary branch, and the collection of the one hundred millionth pound in premiums.

In September of the following year, the management suffered another loss in the death of Philip Smith, a joint managing director. He had been connected with the company for 35 years, during 22 of which he had served as a director. He represented the office on the committee of the Industrial Life Offices Association from 1912 onwards, and from the same year acted as joint treasurer for the National Amalgamated Approved Society. He was a joint general manager for the company from 1909 to 1914, in which year he was appointed joint managing director, a position which he held until his death. He was succeeded by J. Proctor Green.

In 1926 the company was once again called upon to deal with the problem of accumulating arrears, though happily not on the wide scale of five years previously. In May of that year there occurred that unique phenomenon—a general strike; and though this was of short duration, it was followed by a coal strike which lasted for several months. The difficulties thus thrust upon the field force were serious, and were sympathetically regarded by the company, which offered them all possible help in their efforts to maintain their debits. The extent to which recourse was had to the special arrears arrangements was shown in the balance sheet for 1926, when the item " Abatement [of outstanding premiums] to provide *inter alia* for loss of revenue " is shown to have increased during the year by over £172,000.

The strike gave the staff at chief office ample scope for the exercise of determination and initiative to get to work at all. Every variety of transport, suitable or unsuitable, was pressed into service, and probably the only form of conveyance they did not utilise was the ice cream cart, complete with canopy, which was seen to rattle down Oxford Street with six full-grown men filling more than adequately the space usually occupied by the freezers. In addition to walking, other methods of travel included motor charabanc, taxi, car, motor cycle, sidecar, pillion, cycle, step of cycle, tradesman's van and greengrocer's cart, often enough different combinations being employed to complete the journey. One most creditable case was that of three girls from the Glossop district who walked six miles to Hyde, through the two long Hattersley tunnels, on the chance of finding some sort of conveyance to Manchester: which they did. One man was perhaps unfortunate: leaving home at 7.0 a.m. to walk to the office, he was immediately picked up by a motorist, and arrived at the office at 7.20—with not even a newspaper to read.

The palm, however, by general consent, was given to the man who travelled to the office in a hearse.

For some time, the board had been considering the transaction of house purchase business, and in May, 1926, it was resolved that the scheme then prepared be put into operation the following month. It was warmly welcomed by the staff, whose competitive power was thereby increased, and a considerable amount of business was at once introduced. Since that date, the proportion of the company's assets invested in mortgages on house property has materially increased; and, indeed, it has been necessary on occasion to damp down the flow of new business, which, if accepted, would not have been to the advantage of the investment portfolio.

In October, 1926, the Corporation of Manchester conducted what was styled a " Civic Week ". The purpose of the scheme was to advertise to the world what sort of a city Manchester was: the multiplicity and size of the various trades and industries carried on within its boundaries: its ambitions for the future: and its ability to realise them. The week lasted from October 2nd to October 9th; and the Refuge played its part in making it the success it undoubtedly was.

In the first place, a generous contribution was made to the civic week expenses fund. Next, Cyril Clegg, F.I.A., an official of the company, acted as chairman of a sub-committee of tenants of offices in Oxford Street, charged with the duty of devising and carrying out a scheme of street decoration within that area. The office's own contribution to this was to decorate its own frontages with flags and flower boxes: the courtyard with palms and shrubs: to illumine the war memorial: and, most appreciated of all, to floodlight the tower.

One part of the programme was a pageant of industries, which consisted of a parade through the city of a column of lorries each depicting aspects of the work of the principal industries of the district. The Refuge, as representing life assurance, showed two tableaux, one depicting the necessity for whole life assurance, and the other the advantages of endowment assurance. In the latter, a retired married couple was shown in a pleasant house and garden protected by the fence of endowment assurance from the wolves of want and poverty.

It need hardly be said that the wits of chief office affected to believe that the couple were in fact sheltering in the house from the ravening wolves of insurance agents: a jest which the field staff naturally accepted with composure as a tribute to their efficacy as salesmen.

Both tableaux were shown later on a similar occasion in a neighbouring town.

Lastly, the operatic and dramatic society produced a complete panel and episode in the historical pageant in Heaton Park, an achievement equalled by no other society or business house.

During the week over a thousand persons were conducted on tours of inspection of the office, in the course of which there were explained to them the many different activities incident to the work of a life assurance office. Over 40,000 visited the courtyard to view the war memorial.

In 1928, the death occurred of the chairman, Jas. S. Proctor. He had served on the board since 1907, and was appointed joint general manager in 1912. Two years later he became joint managing director, and was elected chairman of the board in 1922, in which capacity he served until his death. He was a member of the original committee of management of the National Amalgamated Approved Society in 1912, and became successively vice-chairman (1920), vice-president (1922), and president (1925). He also represented the office on the executive of the Industrial Life Offices Association from 1922 until his death. He was succeeded as chairman of the Refuge by J. Wilcock Holgate.

In the same year an entirely new step was taken in the industrial branch. In this branch, all the policies were, in form, non-profit; but it was now considered that the company's financial strength had so developed as to justify a distribution of surplus amongst the different groups of policyholders. This was done in some cases by placing permanently upon the latest and most favourable scales of benefit the sums assured under earlier policies, and in others, subject to this maximum, by increasing the sums assured in the event of death within

ROBERT MOSS, J.P.

No. 3 Building, rear view and private roadway

a certain period. A distribution of some sort had been a project for some time and this first allocation of profits remains a landmark in the history of the branch. In view of what has happened since, it is safe to say now that the board had a much more ambitious scheme in mind— the eventual declaration of reversionary bonuses; but such a system necessitates the building up of very large reserves, and it was recognised that it must remain a long-range plan. The first reversionary bonus was in fact declared in 1954.

In 1930 the retirement took place of W. H. Aldcroft, F.I.A. He was the first full-time actuary the company had ever had and he had held the position for 34 years, having also been a general manager since 1914. He was elected to a seat on the board, and S. G. Leigh, F.I.A., was appointed general manager in his place. His position as actuary was entrusted to Cyril Clegg, F.I.A., and at the same time Albert Swift, who had been sole general inspector for some years, was appointed agency manager at chief office.

W. H. Aldcroft died in 1931, the year following his appointment to the board. As the first permanent actuary, he had built up the actuarial side of the company's organisation; and the accountancy system too, was very largely his creation. His term of office as general manager covered 16 very difficult years, including not only the whole of the Great War but also the very difficult period of re-organisation and industrial unrest which followed. He promoted the recruitment of promising young men and kept a sympathetic eye on their progress. He believed in Refuge men having a wide outlook, and encouraged them to take part in affairs outside the office. A man of strong character and quick temper, he coupled with his ability fads and fancies which the staff fully appreciated as good material for the stories about him which still survive. He is affectionately remembered as having been quite unapproachable on a Monday morning if his favourite football club had lost on the preceding Saturday.

The new management team was almost immediately confronted

with a set of problems more difficult than any that had gone before; for the world as a whole had sunk into the worst economic depression ever previously experienced. The preceding five years had been a period of comparative prosperity: but it was an uneasy prosperity and the crisis came following the financial collapse in the United States in 1929. Despite the efforts made to keep the effects within bounds, the international economic situation steadily worsened in 1930; and in 1931, when Great Britain abandoned the gold standard, affairs were at their worst. The company found it necessary to modify the bases of valuation in order to release the very heavy additional amounts which it was necessary to transfer to the investments reserve funds in view of the heavy depreciation in the market value of securities which had occurred during the year. Happily, by the following December the position had very largely been restored; but once again the problem of excess arrears had to be faced. A system known as " part surrenders " was therefore initiated, whereby it was hoped not only to reduce the heavy outstanding arrears to reasonable proportions, but also to maintain a high rate of collection of premiums in the future. Under the scheme, arrears which it was quite clear could not otherwise be reduced were in effect collected by reducing the sum assured by the reversionary equivalent of the premiums outstanding. By the steady application of this system, which naturally called for the most careful supervision both in the field and at chief office, the two objects were attained, and the " excess arrears " figure was reduced to manageable proportions.

During the ten years succeeding the war, the expense ratio in the industrial branch, always a popular target for criticism, had been steadily reduced from the high percentages unavoidable in war conditions to a figure of $36\frac{1}{2}$ per cent, a reduction of over a quarter of the 1920 figure. The process of consolidation in the field, both as regards the number of districts and the total staff, had been completed; and the policy now adopted by the board was so to tighten up administration within that framework as to enable this steady reduction of expenses to be maintained. The result was most successful, the expense ratio by 1939 having been steadily diminished to 32 per cent. A striking illustration of what this drive for economy actually meant is shown by the total figure of savings in expenses which these successive reductions secured within the period 1930–1939 inclusive, amounting to £1,447,661. In the same period the total amount of surplus allocated to the policyholders was £2,239,332, whilst, perhaps most important of all, the valuation bases had been so strengthened as to add very large sums to the life assurance funds held as security for the policy-holders. The day of reversionary bonuses in the industrial branch had been brought appreciably nearer.

Once again the business came to be the subject of inquiry: this time in 1931, when what is known as the Cohen Inquiry was set up as a committee to examine and report on the law and practice relating to industrial assurance. A massive amount of evidence was taken, including a detailed memorandum from the association. Sub-sequently, the association compiled a summary of memoranda prepared by various sub-committees set up to examine and comment upon the evidence given before the main inquiring body. The Refuge was represented on these sub-committees by their solicitor, J. Harrison; their general manager, S. G. Leigh, F.I.A.; and their actuary, Cyril Clegg, F.I.A.

The report was published in 1933, and there was much therein with which the industry could agree: but as Dermot Morrah remarks in his " History of Industrial Life Assurance ", the committee re-peatedly betrayed in their comments that they had misunderstood both the life and needs of the insured population, and the nature of the work the offices were doing to supply their requirements. In so flexible and intimate a business, the long-standing principle of " freedom with publicity " is the basis of the only method whereby the widely varying needs of millions of the populace can be individually met. The separate and independent desires of so large a body of people cannot be satisfied within the framework of a rigid scheme and happily no new legislation emerged as a result of the inquiry. What *did* happen was a strengthening of the resolve of the offices generally to continue their efforts to give more and even better service to their policyholders; and the subsequent experience of the Refuge may be quoted as one example of the success achieved, in that in 1954 in the industrial branch the expense ratio had been reduced to $27\frac{1}{2}$ per cent., the premium income increased from £$5\frac{1}{4}$ millions to £$9\frac{3}{4}$ millions, and the amount allocated to policyholders increased from £150,000 to £1,888,000.

The accommodation at chief office was becoming insufficient to-wards the late 1920s and it was decided to erect a third building on a site the company had purchased some years earlier in Whitworth Street, next to that of No. 1 building; and in 1932 the board authorised the work of erection to begin. Many years earlier the site had been occupied by a firm of timber merchants, containing a canal basin next to where No. 1 building stands to-day. When the foundations were being dug, the old lock gate posts were discovered on the spot where to-day stand the main gates to the private roadway separating nos. 1 and 3 buildings. While the foundations were being put in, interlocking steel piles were driven down to the Red Rock, and reinforced concrete poured in to support the Whitworth Street roadway: when the work was completed the piles were cut off at road level and left *in situ*, this being the economical course. The concrete was faced with glazed brick which can be seen to-day on the wall of the basement.

Some twenty years, and a major war, intervened between 1912, when No. 2 building was opened, and the commencement of work on No. 3. Naturally enough, the building was designed on very different lines by the architect, Stanley Birkett. It consists of seven storeys, constructed of ferro-concrete frame, floors and roof, and is faced with red terra-cotta on the road frontage and with white glazed bricks and buff terra-cotta on the remaining sides. A feature of the upper floors is the total absence of isolated columns, thereby increasing light and space. A large assembly and staff dining hall, 26 feet high, is provided in the two lower floors, together with modern kitchens. At one end is a fully equipped stage, with dressing rooms, for the use of the staff operatic and dramatic societies. On the lower ground floor, there is also a smaller conference hall with a suite of committee rooms. The private roadway, which is entered from Whitworth Street, is extended across the River Medlock by means of a double-deck bridge, and leads to a three-storey steel-framed building which is used for the service departments, the storage of records, and as a garage.

The whole building is modern in conception, even by the standards of to-day, and gives an impression of airiness and light. Functionally, it is the most efficient of the three buildings, probably because of its simplicity of arrangement.

For many years the company has had an extensive joinery department in which all workings in wood, from the simplest to the most elaborate, are carried out. The staff varies from time to time but to-day numbers seven, all skilled men, under a head joiner who is a craftsman in his own right. There are the printers, the engineers, the plumbers, the decorators, the maintenance men, the porters and—after the office closes—the cleaners. All have their allotted space; and all are under the supervision of a departmental head, whose responsibility is that of the building as a whole and its maintenance. There is a resident engineer—whose son represents the third generation of Refuge engineers—and a house steward. Indeed, buildings such as these, and the staffs involved, can well be likened to communities in miniature.

The presiding genius of No. 2 building had been a certain character named C. J. Hargreaves—always referred to as Chris. Hargreaves. He had been the managing clerk for a firm of solicitors which at one time did a considerable amount of work for the company, and in the 1880's he was persuaded to join the Refuge, where—though not a qualified solicitor—he did sound work in legal matters. He was appointed assistant secretary in April, 1888, and adopted the new building as just another of the manifold tasks for which he made himself responsible.

No. 3 building became the charge of J. B. Whitaker, a grandson of the original James Proctor, whose position was that of official in charge of stores, supplies, printing, upkeep of premises, and household staff. His knowledge of building and materials was extensive, and in his careful watch over affairs as a sort of super clerk-of-works was most effective in helping to make the new building the functional success it certainly is, and in keeping an eagle eye on expenses. When he retired in 1951 he left behind him a tradition of efficient administration of household affairs which has been of great service to the company. His name is always associated with No. 3 building, and to this day the private roadway is known as " Whitaker Avenue ".

In 1938 the board resolved to take a further step in the provision of pensions for the staff. Under the scheme set up in 1920, any pensions granted became the liability of the company, and it was now thought advisable to transfer this liability to a superannuation trust fund, to be set up by, and supported by appropriate contributions from, the company, there being again no intention of making the scheme contributory on the part of the staff. A trust was therefore created which was approved under Section 32 of the Finance Act, 1921, divided into two parts:

(a) Employees on the staff as at 31.12.1938, whose benefits were those laid down in the 1920 scheme; and

(b) Employees joining the staff on 1.1.1939 or after, whose benefits were those set out in a new scheme drawn up in the light of more modern conditions.

The annual contributions by the company to support the trust are very heavy, including as they do the amortisation payments to deal with the back-service liabilities in respect of the pre-1939 employees, and they represent a very considerable addition to the cash earnings of the individuals concerned.

For many years the company had been transacting both ordinary and industrial business in Ireland, and in 1934 was operating both in Northern Ireland and in the Irish Free State. In that year the Government of the Free State announced its intention of creating a new company under its control, to transact both life and general insurance; and the Refuge, with all other external offices, would be subject to the provisions of an Act then in course of preparation. After prolonged discussions it became apparent that it was the aim of the Irish Government to take control of the insurance business in the Free State, and it was felt that the potentialities of difficulties arising were so great that the better course would be to retire from the country. The experience generally over the years had been unfavourable, due in the main to a high rate of expense and an adverse mortality experience, and though these unfavourable features were being gradually overcome, the small apparent surpluses did not justify the bonuses actually declared. Accordingly, therefore, following a special resolution of the shareholders on July 4th, 1939, the company's industrial assurance business in Eire was taken over by the Industrial and Life Assurance Amalgamation Company, Limited, of Dublin; and this step was taken in common with other British industrial-ordinary offices. The preliminary negotiations were prolonged and covered a wide field; and in the circumstances the board was satisfied that the transfer was desirable, and that the interests of all parties concerned had been fully protected.

The number of policies taken over was 144,626 with a premium income of £208,540 per annum, occasioning the transfer to the Irish company of funds amounting to £292,074 on account of the liability under the transferred policies which was now undertaken by the Irish Company.

The ordinary branch business in Eire was not transferred. No new business, however, in that country has since been transacted, and the policies then existing have been serviced on the Refuge account by the Irish Assurance Company, Limited.

CHAPTER XII

1939—1945

THE outbreak of the second major war confronted the company not
only with all the problems of the 1914–18 conflict, but also with some
quite different ones, of which no one had had experience, and which
involved consequences the seriousness of which was entirely unpre-
dictable. The circumstances also were very different. The event
did not come upon the country as a surprise: Munich had given notice
of what was to happen, and the Refuge had made preparations to meet
what emergencies could be foreseen, and in co-operation with the
insurance associations had adopted plans in relation to existing policies
and to those which were not yet written. The questions considered
were: (a) maintenance of policies; (b) war claims; (c) investment
difficulties; (d) staff problems; (e) contact with policyholders;
(f) effects of bombing. Each was a major problem in itself, and the
company held itself fortunate in having had time in which to plan
adjustments in its organisation to meet the new conditions.

The maintenance of policies was not this time merely a matter of
the financial ability of the policyholders to continue the payment of
the premiums. With the probable dispersals among the population,
it seemed very likely that the real difficulty would be actually to *find*
the policyholders; and the manner in which this was contrived is set out
below. As regards the maintenance of premium payments the
opportunity was taken of exploring thoroughly how best this could be
arranged: not only the offices themselves but the Industrial Assurance

EVACUATED PERSONS

who are

POLICYHOLDERS of the

REFUGE

ASSURANCE COMPANY LIMITED

or whose

NATIONAL HEALTH INSURANCE

is administered by the "REFUGE" should call immediately at the Company's District Office, so that arrangements to give them service again may be made

DO NOT DELAY!

The District Office for this locality is:

Notice to Evacuated Policyholders

Bomb Damage: Southampton Office, before and after

Commissioner also were enabled, as practical people, to put forward and discuss various suggestions, and the result was the Industrial Assurance and Friendly Societies (Emergency Protection from Forfeiture) Act, 1940, which proved a much more satisfactory means of effecting the desired end than that provided by similar legislation during the 1914–18 war. Generally speaking, policies which were in force just before September 1st, 1939, for sums assured not exceeding £50 on which at least two years' premiums had been paid, came under the provisions for protection against forfeiture on application by the owners, and these provisions were interpreted very liberally by the company. An appeal could always be made to the Commissioner, but comparatively few policyholders exercised this right.

The problem of war claims was also a double one, involving not only existing policies, which fully covered civilian war risks whilst excluding those arising out of service in the armed forces, but also future policies which might involve not only men in the Services, as in 1914–1918, but also civilians amongst whom it was feared very heavy casualties would arise as a result of attacks on this country. In the event, it was resolved to pay in full, for the time being, all claims arising in respect of existing policies, a concession which in fact was continued throughout the war; whilst in respect of contracts taken out after it began, the company subscribed to the agreement arrived at between the offices in the associations whereby limited life assurance cover was provided both for service personnel and civilians who met their deaths directly or indirectly as a result of war. Claims in respect of other deaths were paid as usual. The effect of war conditions on new business was much less than might have been expected, as is shown by the figures on the next page:

New Business

Year	Ordinary Branch			Industrial Branch	
	No. of Policies	Sums Assured	Annual Premiums	No. of Policies	Sums Assured
1938	50, 744	7,894,878	434,655	838,675	15,861,062
1939	41,926	6,422,725	361,865	748,643	14,325,779
1942	36,620	7,027,047	426,380	526,574	11,763,229
1945	27,550	5,996,392	384,410	364,757	8,742,095
1946	42,831	11,516,078	665,915	440,861	11,754,765
1947	48,904	15,917,943	919,870	448,898	13,201,100

The table indicates how effectively the field staff—many of them quite inexperienced at the outset—maintained the company's life assurance services. Not only was the number of new policies most creditable, but clearly, in the increase in the average sum assured, there was appreciation of the fall in the value of money. The figures suggest, too, a certain transfer of interest from the industrial to the ordinary branch, a consequence, no doubt, of the higher earnings arising as a result of war conditions.

The financial problems were considerable. Opportunities for investment were severely limited, and as regards new money, the company joined with the industry generally in supporting Government loans by way of savings bonds, which were on tap. The low yield on these transactions, consequent on the Government's cheap money policy, coupled with the increases in costs of all forms of expenditure, had their effect on the surpluses available for distribution, and it was therefore decided to pay bonuses at reduced rates in the ordinary branch and only on policies which became claims during each year in question. The undistributed surpluses were put to reserve in the hope —which was in fact realised—of utilising them in due course to declare reversionary bonuses to existing policies in respect of each of the war years.

The staff problems had to be faced at once. It is true that the experience of the early days of 1914–18 was not repeated, when enlistment centres all over the country were unable to cope with the throngs of men rushing to volunteer. Volunteers there were in plenty, of course, but in general it was desired by the authorities that men—and in this war, women—should remain at their posts until called up. Nevertheless, the immediate loss of all Reservists and Territorials, coupled with the volunteers and the first men and women called up for national service, created gaps—especially in the field staff—which once again had to be filled by those too old for service, by pensioners, by women: and well indeed they contrived, inexperienced though many of them were. At the end of 1939, there were six full-time female agents; the next year 1,853; and in 1941, 3,076—over fifty per cent. of the entire agency force. Both in the field and at chief office, the total numbers employed were progressively reduced—the former by 20 per cent., the latter by over one-third. As in 1914–18, all those who were called up for service with the Armed Forces were guaranteed re-employment on their return—though on this occasion it was made a statutory obligation—and the company undertook to make up their service remuneration to one-half, two-thirds or the whole of their weekly salary, within certain limits dependent on their domestic circumstances. Somewhat similar grants were made to full-time female employees called up for national service.

Maintenance of contact with policyholders was indeed, in many cases, a difficult business. What with the evacuation schemes, the prohibited areas, the dispersals consequent on bombing, the sleeping in air-raid shelters, the departures to the various services: the servicing of the debits seemed almost impossible. But it was not so. In all areas where there were likely to be evacuated Refuge policyholders, leaflets were distributed giving the address of the local office; whilst, in addition, posters were exhibited in public halls, schools, billeting offices, etc., giving the same information. All policyholders were urged to travel with their premium receipt books, and the instances were few indeed where they failed to be contacted by Refuge personnel in the areas in which they found their temporary habitations.

But the majority of people did not move at all—except at night; when they repaired to air-raid shelters, tube stations, office basements, tunnels and similar places of supposed—though relative—safety. The evening is, of course, a normal time for collection of industrial branch premiums, and the most enterprising and ingenious methods were adopted by the agents to carry this out. They were quick to discover in which shelters their members were accustomed to sleep, and it was a normal occurrence in London for policyholders to take with them on certain nights their premium receipt books together with the premiums ready for their agent to collect. How often was the call heard in various shelters; " Any Refuge policyholders here? "

As one London Superintendent has described it: "All through the period, collections were excellent, and the new female staff really wonderful. Each one knew where the policyholder would be whatever time 'Wailing Winnie' went, and the collections continued in whatever shelters were available in the areas ". Indeed, often enough, alternative addresses were the order of the day, and many debits were arranged in " air-raid shelter order " and not " house and street order ". If an office was out of action, alternative accommodation was found—even in basements. And throughout, each man took his turn at firewatching at night, or acting as warden wherever his home might be.

Of the company's local offices, one hundred were damaged by bombs in one degree or another, some twice, thrice or even four times.

Gt. Yarmouth, Swansea, Southampton, Greenock and Southwark were totally destroyed. Following the Clydebank raids of March, 1941, it was months before agencies recovered, and in fact some debit was never heard of again. Gt. Yarmouth was bombed in daylight on February 18th, 1942, on paying-in day, and the superintendent, W. J. Parnell, his wife (a temporary agent), assistant Parminter and the clerk, Miss Holmes, were all killed.

Chief office escaped lightly, even in the blitz in December, 1940, which destroyed so much of the centre of the city. Many incendiaries struck the building, but no serious fire resulted. At different times blast damage was experienced, but the only ill-effects were to slates and windows. Fire patrols were formed as early as 1938, and male members of the staff were made up into teams of eight (later increased to 16) with a leader to each team. They took over in turn after office hours and were on duty throughout the night. One man in each team took over the office of cook: some teams were lucky and others not so fortunate. Two air-raid shelters were built, one in the basement of No. 2 building for the staff, and another off the dining hall in No. 3 building, for the use of the public. The blast walls and steel work still remain.

The public shelter provided accommodation for from 300–400 people, and many of these became regular tenants. One visitor was a woman who, after being discharged from St. Mary's Hospital opposite, after the birth of her baby, came regularly each night for shelter, her husband being in the Auxiliary Fire Service. The child was a great favourite with the fire squads, who christened him "Jimmy Refuge" and amused him by wheeling him up and down the dining hall, on one of the service trollies. He is a big fine fellow to-day.

One of the fears of the management was that chief office might be destroyed, and with it the main records. No department was actually evacuated *en bloc*; but, wherever possible, records were duplicated and dispatched to some place away from Manchester for—it was hoped—

safe storage. An outstanding example is that of the several hundred thousands of ordinary branch record cards in the actuarial department which were duplicated throughout and sent up to the Kendal office in Westmorland, where they constituted a reserve set of records which were " worked " in similar fashion to those retained in Oxford Street,

Many machines at chief office depended entirely on electric power; and to overcome the consequences of breakdowns in the main supply, an entirely independent generating set was installed in the basement which, in an emergency, could be set in motion not only to supply a modified degree of illumination but also sufficient power to keep the machinery in operation. As a result, not once was chief office out of action, even in part. With the additional work thrown upon them, the machines were worked extremely hard, and the staffs were, on occasion, on duty in the office throughout the entire week-end. It is to be wondered what the pioneers, with their nonconformist background, would have thought of Sunday working.

In January, 1944, the death occurred of J. Proctor Green. He had been connected with the company for 46 years, having first joined the service in 1898. He was a grandson of the original James Proctor, and the son of R. W. Green, a former chairman. He passed through the various departments in chief office, and in 1914 was appointed general manager, jointly with W. H. Aldcroft, with whom he acted until his appointment as managing director in 1925, jointly with Jas. S. Proctor. He had previously been elected to the board in 1922, and was appointed deputy chairman in 1928. His main interest was in investments, of which he had made a long study and which he operated on behalf of the company with conspicuous success. He represented the Refuge in London from 1922 onwards, being elected a member of the executive committee of the Industrial Life Offices Association in that year, later becoming deputy chairman (1928) and vice-chairman (1932): also serving as a member of the committee of management of the National Amalgamated Approved Society (1922) and later as joint treasurer (1932). A quiet man and thoughtful, his views were expressed only after reflection and then with authority; and they were received always with respect.

In his relations with his colleagues and with the staffs, he was held—and his memory still is to-day—in a quite remarkable affection. He had a gift for seeing the other man's point of view and meeting him as far as possible—a quality which enabled him on the proper occasions to say "No" and to have the decision accepted without question or rancour. He shared with W. H. Aldcroft the cares of management during the first Great War and its troublous aftermath: it is sad to reflect that in his closing years he had once again to cope with similar problems.

CHAPTER XIII

Industrial Assurance and Politics

BEVERIDGE REPORT: NATIONAL INSURANCE ACT, 1946:
INDUSTRIAL ASSURANCE AND FRIENDLY SOCIETIES ACT, 1948:
ANTI-NATIONALISATION CAMPAIGN: INDUSTRIAL ASSURANCE
COUNCIL.

LOOKING well ahead, the Government as far back as 1941 had arranged for a comprehensive survey of existing schemes of social insurance and allied services which were later to be considered by the committee on reconstruction problems; and an interdepartmental committee was set up to conduct this survey under the chairmanship of Sir William Beveridge. Although at the outset industrial assurance was not within the ambit of the inquiry, it was later drawn in by a Government announcement that the committee would have power to consider the addition of death benefits under the national insurance schemes. As matters of high policy came to be involved, it was not proper for the departmental representatives, as civil servants, to remain as members of the committee, and they therefore merely acted as advisers and assessors to Sir William, who alone was responsible for the recommendations in the report.

Evidence was given by representatives of the Industrial Life Offices Association, to which the Refuge contributed; and the business as a whole was referred to in the report in a separate Appendix entitled, rather oddly, " The problem of industrial assurance ". In view of the continued progress of the offices and the effective service, both in extent and quality, they were rendering their policyholders, the wording might perhaps appear to be tendentious. It is curious,

J. Proctor Green, J.P.

J. Wilcock Holgate

too, to read Sir William as writing " it cannot be admitted that weekly collection of premiums is a permanent indispensable requirement for securing voluntary contributions from persons of limited means ". As regards voluntary as opposed to compulsory contributions, history—and human nature—was against him: for example, in the Post Office Insurance Scheme, which failed for lack of collectors; in the national savings campaign during the war, which found door-to-door and personal collections essential; and in the success of the Refuge Friend in Deed and other offices which emerged from the jungle of failures a hundred years before simply because there *was* adopted the policy of home collection. How far is the academic mind removed from the world and human nature!

In the consideration of reconstruction problems after the war, two suggestions in the report affecting industrial assurance offices were adopted by the Government, i.e., the taking over of the approved societies by the Ministry of National Insurance, and the inclusion of a death benefit in the new scheme of national insurance. Provisions to this effect were included in the National Insurance Act, 1946.

In 1948 there was passed yet another statute affecting the business, the Industrial Assurance and Friendly Societies Act, 1948, which withdrew generally the powers formerly granted to insure for funeral expenses within certain permitted relationships. With the exception of husband and wife, each of whom is presumed to have an insurable interest in the life of the other, the only permissible life-of-another assurance for funeral expenses is now that on a parent, step-parent or grandparent; and then only for a sum not exceeding £20. [Now increased to £30 by the Industrial Assurance and Friendly Societies r948 (Amendment) Act, 1958.]

The effect of both statutes on the operations of the Refuge was slight. As regards the dissolution of the approved societies it was on grounds of sentiment rather than of finance that it was a source of regret to the office to cease the personal and friendly service to the members in their homes rendered by the field staff during so many years; and all employees engaged wholly on national health work were offered the opportunity to remain with the company if they did not wish to enter the service of the new Ministry. With very few exceptions they preferred to remain with the company.

The post-war years induced a political climate different from any other that had previously prevailed. It was the era of the welfare state, of nationalisation; and in 1949 the Party in power issued a statement containing the proposal " that all the industrial assurance companies and the larger collecting societies should be taken over as they stand ". The proposal was so plainly contrary to the best interests of everyone concerned, whether the community as a whole, the policy-holders or the staffs, that the offices took immediate advantage of the invitation of the Party to discuss the statement as widely as possible, with particular reference to industrial assurance. The Refuge began by holding a Press conference at chief office, in the course of which the managers made plain the attitude of the industry and the reasons therefor, and answered the questions addressed to them by the Press representatives. Subsequently, a series of staff meetings was held at chief office and throughout the country, on non-political lines, at which the secretary, M. Wilcock Holgate, or one of the general managers, Cyril Clegg, F.I.A., or E. G. Almond, dealt with nationalisation from the point of view of the practical men there assembled. In particular, it was pointed out that the Party in power was wrong in referring to the proposal as a major recommendation of Sir William. It was *not:* as his report plainly states. Certainly it would have been convenient to take over the business with its trained staff; and the machinery of the offices would have been most useful in the operation of the main scheme. But administrative convenience is no reason for the destruction of a service which is essentially personal, and which exists to meet an infinite diversity of needs and financial capacities. No statutory body, with its inherent inflexibility of operation, could do the same.

That was certainly the view of the Refuge staff, who were overwhelmingly opposed to the idea.

For many years there had been in existence a body styled the " Industrial Assurance Council " on which members of the association worked in close co-operation with the Prudential Assurance Company in what might be described as public relations work, and publicity generally. It was obviously desirable for the public to be well acquainted with the facts relating to the industry; and accordingly the council, with its local committees, numbering over 400, has since 1950 been engaged in a continuous goodwill campaign which has gone far to correct the misapprehensions which were so commonplace a few years ago.

The Refuge was originally represented on the council by J. Wilcock Holgate, whose place has now been taken by his son, Maurice, the present managing director of the company.

CHAPTER XIV

Modern Developments

MODERN WAYS: GRANT OF ARMS: FIRST PRESIDENT: WAR
MEMORIAL PLAQUE: LETTING OF NO. 3 BUILDING: ENTRY INTO
GENERAL INSURANCE: LONDON INVESTMENT OFFICE: QUOTATION
ON STOCK EXCHANGE: MECHANISATION: PUBLICITY: RECON-
STRUCTION OF CAPITAL.

A HUNDRED years is a long time; and with such long established
business concerns, especially with a strong family element such as has
distinguished the Refuge, there is always the risk of a tendency to
become old-fashioned—to become set in one's ways. This has been
carefully avoided in Oxford Street; and, indeed, within the last few
years the company has taken up progressive ideas which would have
done credit to a young firm bursting with modernity. They will be
mentioned in their chronological order.

From the very early days the sign of the office had been a bee hive:
hence came the idea of the glass bees on the faces of the clock in the
tower. It was now felt that the time had arrived to adopt armorial
bearings as being more in keeping with the magnitude and importance
of the concern, and on September 28th, 1951, the patent granting the
arms was formally received by the chairman on behalf of the board.

The blazoning or heraldic description reads:

" Gules a Beehive Or on a chief Azure a pair of scales between a tower and a garb
of the second. Crest: on a wreath of the colours a representation of Noah's Ark
proper. Supporters: Dexter the figure of a woman representing Justice proper blind-
folded and habited in a robe Argent in the dexter hand a pair of scales and in the other
a Sword erect Or sinister a Lion guardant Gules murally crowned and charged on
the shoulder with a Rose Or Motto *Refugium rebus adversis* ".

The various " charges " or symbols represent the ideals and

objects of the office. The BEEHIVE suggests industry in service to policyholders and has formed part of the company's seal since inception, as also have the SCALES OF JUSTICE occupying the centre of the shield. The GOLD TOWER indicates strength, and the WHEATSHEAF is taken from the County Arms of Cheshire, the county in which the first head office of the company was situate in Dukinfield. The ARK represents protection, and is incorporated in the design over the entrance to the first chief office in Oxford Street, Manchester. The SUPPORTERS are Justice and a Guardian Lion, the latter taken from the Manchester City Arms, representing the guardianship offered. The CROWN worn by the Lion is a heraldic civic crown which identifies it with the City. The GOLD ROSE on the Lion's shoulder represents England, and the County Palatine of Lancaster with which the company has for so long been associated.

The motto *Refugium Rebus Adversis*—" a refuge in times of trouble " (Psalm 9v.9)—stresses not only the motif of the arms and a pun or rebus on the company's name, but also the intentions and principles upon which the office has always acted.

In April, 1952, J. Wilcock Holgate relinquished his position as chairman, and was succeeded by Wm. Proctor Smith, J.P. In recognition of Mr. Holgate's services to the company during his 24 years as chairman of the board, he was invited by his colleagues to accept the appointment as the company's first president, an invitation which he accepted.

His services with the company extended over a very long period. He was first employed as office boy in the Blackburn office in 1895, and passed through every department there. He had experience of field work, at one time holding an agency, and subsequently becoming assistant inspector. He was appointed to the board in 1912, at the same time assuming control of the Blackburn division, the largest of the director-areas. In 1926 he was appointed the first deputy chairman of the company; and finally, in 1928, its chairman. He played an important part in the administration of the industrial assurance business as a whole. For many years he was a member of the executive committee of the association, and later became its vice-president: during the war he served on numerous committees set up to deal with problems affecting the business under the then conditions. He was an original member of the Industrial Assurance Council. He assisted in the formation of the National Amalgamated Approved Society in 1912, and as joint treasurer served on the committee of management from 1925, becoming chairman of the society in 1936, a position which he retained until the taking over of the Approved Societies in 1948—practically for one-third of the lifetime of the society. He was also chairman of the National Conference of Industrial Assurance Approved Societies.

On September 16th, 1949, he was entertained to a luncheon by his colleagues to mark the completion of 21 years as chairman of the company, to which there were invited to meet him over 400 other guests representative of every area in which the Refuge carried on operations, and of every grade of employee both in chief office and in the field, in whose welfare he had taken so great an interest for so long a time.

His death occurred in 1955, after a period of service extending over 60 years.

For some considerable time much thought had been given as to how best to inscribe upon the existing war memorial the company's tribute to those members of the staff who lost their lives in combat in the second Great War. It was not felt proper to modify in any way the dedicatory column of the original memorial; and it was therefore decided to set into the steps of the plinth, in a stone similar to that of the monument, a cast bronze plaque bearing the figures " 1939–1945 " and the names of the 112 fallen, this to become an integral part of the memorial itself. To quote the " In Memoriam " booklet: " The winged Victory, raised above, with palm and laurel wreath, stands to unite in everlasting memory those whose names are written at her feet ".

The dedication ceremony was carried out on May 21st, 1953, attended by members of the board and management, and by representatives of the staffs. The service was conducted by the Reverend Canon F. Paton-Williams, and the plaque was unveiled by the chairman of the company, Wm. Proctor Smith, J.P.

No. 3 building was begun in 1932, not only to relieve the then congestion in the other buildings, but also to provide for the anticipated future expansion of staff and the need for storage space. Events, however, did not turn out quite as was expected, for several reasons. The number of new policies issued in the industrial branch had diminished, as also had the number of discontinuances, due no doubt to the improved financial status of the industrial classes; whilst the development of office machinery enabled a smaller staff to deal with an increased amount of work. As a result there was space to spare; and since space in a city is a valuable commodity, it was resolved to accept one of the many offers to take over part of the new building. Fortunately, only part of the premises were let: for a need soon arose for the remaining floors to be utilised on the company's behalf.

It has been recorded that as long ago as 1920, the question of entry into the field of general insurance had been discussed. Indeed, the idea goes back to an even earlier date, for in 1865 it had been resolved to commence a fire branch, a resolution which was repeated the following year. Nothing seems to have emerged from these resolutions, just as in 1920 the idea was allowed to lie on the table. It was now felt, however, that the company was in a position to venture upon this new field; and long discussions took place as to the most efficient means of carrying out this purpose. In the event, in 1953, an arrangement was entered into with the Federated Employers' Insurance Association, Ltd., whereby the Refuge purchased the entire share capital of the Association, and made use of its organisation to reinsure whatever general business was secured by Refuge personnel, the Federated itself continuing its own operations precisely as before. The Refuge became represented on the board of the Association; and the offices of general manager and deputy general manager of the latter were assumed respectively by the joint general and deputy assistant manager of the former. The respective field staffs work in concert and the combination has no doubt had a beneficial effect on the volume of business transacted by the Association, as may be seen in the following figures:

Year		Net Premium Income
1953	..	£895,259
1957	..	£1,569,302

Although the head office of the Association was in the centre of Manchester, it was clearly advisable that it should be removed to the Refuge offices, from which it was, in fact, to be controlled. Fortunately, there was sufficient accommodation remaining available in No. 3 building, and in November, 1953, the move was completed, so that now both Refuge and Federated are under the same roof.

Despite the excellence to-day of specialised telephonic communication, there is no doubt that it is a very real advantage for any investment concern to have permanent representation in London, the centre of the financial world. With the enormous funds in the charge of the company, it was felt that the investments should be in the hands of specialists, who should be operating at the heart of affairs, and it was therefore resolved on June 25th, 1953, to take an office in the City of London, and to transfer there one of the two investment secretaries together with two of the company's actuaries to assist him in his work. The move has proved entirely successful, the board now being in a position to receive immediate and informed advice upon which they may act with speed and complete confidence. There is no doubt that a great part of the increase in the net yields on both the ordinary and industrial life assurance funds has been due to the carrying out of this—from the standpoint of pre-war years—revolutionary idea.

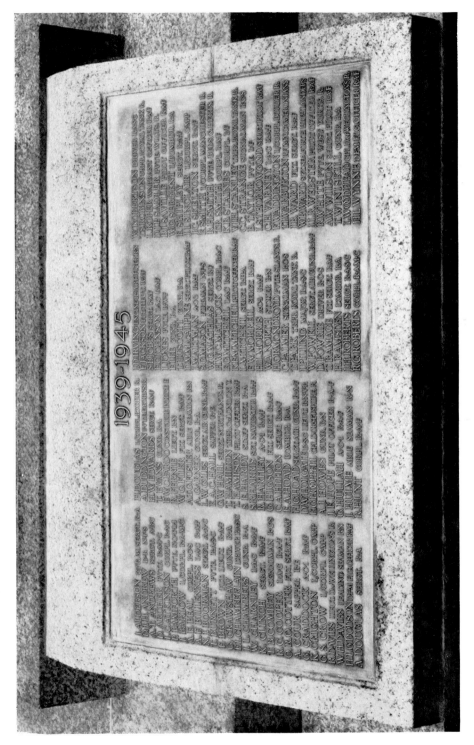

War Memorial Plaque

To All and Singular

Grant of Arms

Although the Refuge had advertised for many years, it is to be doubted whether it did any more than keep its name mildly before the public. It was felt that something more forceful and productive was required; and once again the office found from within its own ranks just the man for the job. Though it can hardly claim credit for putting him on the staff with this specific task in mind, at least it can be said with satisfaction that he was found and given the opportunity to exercise his flair in this particular connection. Things are very different now from the days when some layman on the staff was instructed to prepare a leaflet—which he did with complete accuracy and probably surpassing dullness. To-day there is a special publicity department within chief office where all the jargon of the printer and the advertising man is to be heard; where all forms of leaflets, posters, advertising matter, etc., are devised, and later printed, often in colour, on the machines to be found in the department. Contacts are maintained with all branches of the Press, and advertising is now a continuous and country-wide process, assisted periodically by systematic campaigns.

A feature of these modern days is the increasing degree in which use is made of office machinery. A bare fifty years ago letters were written by hand, and copied in the copying press; arithmetical processes—addition, subtraction, multiplication and division—were a matter for mental ability; tens of thousands of cards were sorted by hand—a tedious job which the juniors were wont to relieve by adventuring how big they could make a pile before it tumbled over; and accounting was a matter of meticulous pen and ink entries in voluminous ledgers. There is nothing of that drudgery to-day: mechanisation has seen to that.

The process has been going on steadily for fifty years. Up to about 1907, the office aids had comprised the copying press, the typewriter (probably one!), and the telephone. Then the first calculating machine was installed—an arithmometer—a cumbersome piece of machinery which performed multiplications and divisions at the expense of quite a degree of manual labour. It was very much of a show piece for some years, and any actuarial clerk chosen to exhibit its operation to visitors was most gratified with his brief hour of importance.

The year 1913 was the initiator of a series of mechanical aids. The machines, and their purposes, ran roughly as follows: calculating and adding (1913); addressing and cheque writing (1914); sorting and tabulation of punched cards (1921); printing on continuous stationery (1925); new means of calculating and adding (1928–31); document photography (1938); alternative punched cards (1939); accounting (1950); folding and enveloping, micro-filming, recorder and reader (1952); rotaprint and composing (1953–4); postal franking ($\frac{1}{2}$d. to 9s. 11$\frac{1}{2}$d.) (1955); and finally, the first introduction of machines into the company's district offices by the trial installation of adding and listing instruments (1957). It is on record that the initial operation of the punched card system in 1921 immediately rendered redundant seventeen clerks—who, of course, were very soon absorbed in the natural growth of the business—and it is an intriguing thought as to how possibly clerical work could now be carried on without these developments of the modern age. Truly it may be said that the need creates the machine.

It has already been remarked that quite soon after its foundation the Refuge became a family concern in that not only the work itself but also the controlling interests became the province of a number of individuals whose successors carried on in their place. Some very large shareholdings came to be built up, which tended to become unwieldy; and it was thought wise to broaden the basis of ownership by putting the shares on the market, which meant, of course, obtaining a Stock Exchange quotation. Application was therefore made to the Stock Exchange in 1955; and the necessary requirements having been complied with, a quotation was authorised on June 27th in that year.

Immediately prior to this step being taken, it was resolved at an extraordinary general meeting on March 31st, 1955, that a reconstruction of capital should be carried out. Ever since the " Friend in Deed " had been converted into a company, the shares had been of the denomination of £2, and had risen in number to 150,000, representing an issued and paid-up capital of £300,000. In order to make the shares more marketable, it was resolved that each of the 150,000 shares should be sub-divided into one "A" ordinary share of £1 fully paid, and two " B " ordinary shares of 10s. each fully paid. Further, that the capital of the company be increased to £600,000 by the creation of 150,000 additional " A " ordinary shares of £1 each and 300,000 additional " B " ordinary shares of 10s. each.

Far indeed had the Refuge travelled from its inception in 1858 with a modest capital of £22 12s. 6d. What a world of work, worry and development is contained within those hundred years!

CHAPTER XV

The Pioneers

It is perhaps only fitting that this history should close with a tribute to the pioneers who worked so ably to transform the Refuge from its status as an indigent burial society to that of an important industrial assurance company, strong and progressive; and with some reference to those presently charged with the task of carrying on that process of development.

The fate and fortunes of the original members of the embryo company varied. Some died; some gave up what must have seemed, at times, a hopeless struggle; and some endured. Of these last, the names of James Proctor and George Robins are pre-eminent.

The name of James Proctor has come down through the years as indicating a personage who, for a long time, was almost the Refuge itself. He must have been a remarkable character, for though he was never formally the chairman of the new company, nor was he even its senior member, it is apparent throughout the records that he was the real force behind the scenes. One gains the impression that the Refuge was his whole life and interest—and it is certain that his influence was felt for good in a much wider field, in the industry as a whole.

Born in Preston in 1820, he originally combined the occupations of general agent and journeyman tailor, in the pursuit of which he would naturally travel over a wide area. His wife came from Keswick, which probably explains why later the society had business in such then remote places as Ulverston, Allithwaite, Cartmel and Staveley, country areas which a travelling tailor might well include in journeys between Preston and Keswick. About 1863 he moved to Manchester, where from his home at 45 Livesey Street, he held together the remains of the old society and in 1864 was one of the principal movers in its incorporation under the Companies Act of 1862. Always retiring, he did not put himself forward to be general manager, a position which went to George Bridge of " Pim Hole Club " fame. It was only after Bridge's death about 1872 that James Proctor assumed the governing position of general manager and managing director, in which capacity he later served under the chairmanship of his son William from 1884 until his death in 1888.

George Robins was invaluable as a secretary in the early days. Whatever his occupation when he lived in Hart Street, Manchester, we soon find him established as a grocer and corn dealer in Broadbottom, near Mottram, having apparently taken over the business from his deceased brother Joe. As the owner of a prosperous business he was independent of the future of the Friend in Deed, and he was able to give to the society care and attention unpressed by events, which must have been most effective. He never afterwards relinquished his business, a circumstance which not only maintained his freedom of action, but enabled him to dip into his own pocket and finance the society when occasion demanded. He continued in the secretaryship until his death in 1871.

The vacant position does not appear to have been filled for some years, the minutes of meetings being the responsibility of Henry Bridge, for subsequent writing up by Robert Moss, who was eventually formally appointed secretary in 1884. The name of Moss is prominent in this connection, as Robert's sister had been the wife of the first secretary, George Robins. Robert himself was the son of a local schoolmaster and shopkeeper in the village of Charlesworth in Derbyshire. His early years were spent working for the Refuge during the day and helping in the shop in the evening. Transport to Dukinfield was by pony and trap, a considerable journey of ten miles each way which must have been very trying in the hard winters of that district. Like James Proctor, he was devoted to the Refuge and its service, which came to be his life. A strict though kindly man, and devout, he was held in high esteem by those who knew him. He served as a director from 1884 until his resignation in 1923, having been a Justice of the Peace for the County of Derbyshire for many years. His death occurred in 1924; and he was succeeded as director and secretary by his son, John W. Moss, who in turn held the position for the next 22 years until his death in January, 1946. A lovable man, he followed the example of his father in giving faithful and long service to the company, extending over a period of 58 years.

While James Proctor was busying himself in the Manchester area, there were similar men with similar thoughts working for the same end in other parts of the country. One of these was Henry Adams, who was born at Hollins End near Sheffield, on March 3rd, 1836, the youngest of a large family who, at the age of nine, commenced work in a Yorkshire coal mine. His family, to improve their circumstances, moved frequently, living at Masborough, Intake and Wombwell Main Colliery, near Barnsley. Henry Adams had none of the educational advantages enjoyed by the youth of to-day, but like so many of the early Refuge members, he was a devoted Methodist and received his early training at Sunday School. He was a thoughtful man, and working in the mines under the conditions of those days, the need of the working man to save and protect himself and his family against the misfortunes of accident, disease and death was very apparent to him. By the time he left the mines at the age of 27 in 1863 to join forces with James Proctor, he had already begun to form his own little local society in South Yorkshire; and in the years which followed until his death in 1906, he successfully developed the business of the Refuge not only in South Yorkshire, but in the counties of Derby, Lincoln and Nottingham, while his son William Adams pioneered the business in the Birmingham area.

Meanwhile, to the south and west of Manchester, in Cheshire and the neighbouring counties, the society's interests were in the keeping of the Thornton family. Henry Thornton was born in Warrington in 1840, the only son of a miller. Apprenticed by his father to a firm of tool-makers, he completed his indentures and immediately branched out on his own as an estate agent and auctioneer. So successful was he in the profession of his choosing that while still a youth he was entrusted with the management of several large estates in the area. His energy appears to have been considerable, for in 1862, while continuing to run his own business, he accepted an agency with the Refuge Friendly Society which, in fact, involved the opening-up of a whole new area of the society's activities. His venture in this realm was by no means to the liking of his family or his friends, for there is no doubt that at that particular period the fortunes of the society were extremely low.

Henry Thornton, however, had a confidence which defied other opinions and time proved his faith amply justified. In the years that followed he developed the Refuge interests in South Lancashire, Cheshire, the Isle of Man, Ireland, and the whole of Wales with the exception of Glamorgan, even infiltrating into parts of the west country, despite the severe difficulties of travel in those days and of language in some of these areas. In 1872 he joined the board of directors.

A deeply religious and conscientious man, albeit with a forceful character, he was a Primitive Methodist until, becoming dissatisfied with them, he and a number of his friends left the chapel and founded a new one, known as the Ebenezer Chapel, in Buttermarket Street, Warrington. In politics he was a Liberal and served for a time on the town council at Warrington where he was also a Justice of the Peace.

As chairman of the Lancashire and Cheshire Band of Hope Union, being himself a non-smoker and total abstainer, he played a sincere and very active part in combating the alcoholic excesses of his generation. He died in 1920 at the age of eighty, having resigned from the board the previous year. He had served the company for fifty-seven years and seen his early faith in its success justified.

Born at Oswaldtwistle, Lancashire, in 1839, Thomas Shutt, schooling over, entered the family cotton mill of J. &. J. Shutt. After serving his apprenticeship he left them to secure improved positions in other branches of the textile business until in 1877, at the age of 38, he abandoned cotton for insurance and took a superintendency with the Refuge in South and West Lancashire which he later extended to parts of Westmorland, Cumberland and Yorkshire. His success was rewarded in 1884 by appointment to the board, on which he continued to serve until his death in 1903 at the age of 64. His political and religious persuasions conformed to those of his colleagues; he was a Liberal and a Wesleyan.

James Wilcock was born in Accrington in 1846 and at an early age was apprenticed to his father, William Wilcock, a skip and basket manufacturer at King Street, Blackburn, who had moved there from Preston in 1854. William, it would seem, had an agency with the Refuge from its earliest days, but took comparatively little interest in it. Son James, however, had other ideas, and after completing his apprenticeship gave more and more of his time to the agency until in 1868, he was appointed district manager for Blackburn. In 1882 the growth of this district justified a move to new offices in Montague Street, Blackburn, and seven years later to 56 Ainsworth Street, the site of the company's present premises. From the one office in King Street he extended the society's and later the company's business, first to Preston and then through North-East Lancashire and the North and West Ridings of Yorkshire, so that 40 years later, in 1908, he controlled a staff of over 1,000 in nearly 50 districts. Having joined the board in 1884, he became its chairman in 1898, a position he held until his death thirteen years later. Like Shutt and the others he was a Liberal and a Wesleyan.

How these men, scattered over what in those days was a wide area, met and joined forces can, for the most part, be only conjecture; but it is reasonable to suppose that James Proctor, the journeyman tailor

The Present Board

James Proctor-Pearson

S. G. Leigh

Richard C. Green

Cyril Clegg

Wm. Proctor Smith

M. Wilcock Holgate

James A. Booth

Francis H. Thornton

from Preston, should, in the course of his normal travels, meet Thomas Shutt, from the cotton mill at Oswaldtwistle, and William Wilcock, basket maker in his own town.

Of his first meetings with Adams of Sheffield and Thornton of Warrington there is, unfortunately, no record. They were, however, all ardent Methodists, some of them lay-preachers, and it may well be that their connection in business began with their contact through the church. Suffice it to say, however, that these were the men who came together and laid the foundations of the company, each of whom in his own sphere and fashion is entitled to be called a founder of what was and always has been a " family " business in the broadest sense, not only to those who claim blood relationship to these men but to the many others who in different capacities have served the company through the years, and been followed in its service by their children and their children's children.

Envoi

LOOKING back over this history, the impression is not only that of a worth-while work having been done extremely well, but also that of a good deal of fun in the doing of it. Until the outbreak of the first Great War in 1914, with no radio, TV, talkies or transport, the rule was a 5½-day—and often enough, a 6-day—week. Hours of work were long, and leisure time very limited; amusements were largely personally organised—there was much pleasure in very simple things, such as singing around the family piano in the evenings; and people were very independent, whether in thought, speech or choice of occupation. To have been a part of a concern such as the Refuge, which very soon after its birth gave promise of a brilliant future, must have been exciting and satisfying: and there is ample evidence of this in the opinions held by those many pensioners of the office who worked for it in years gone by, and who look back on their careers with a feeling that they took part in a great campaign which produced results which gave them pride; and which will grow still more impressive as the years go on. As one famous field man was wont to say:

" THE BEST IS YET TO BE "

Appendix A

The Present Board

WILLIAM PROCTOR SMITH, J.P., is a great-grandson of the Founder. Born in 1891, he was educated at Bowdon College and joined the company in 1910, beginning in the actuarial department, and in 1913 becoming clerk-in-charge of the Manchester and Warrington Divisions in chief office. He was elected to the board in 1922, and in 1925 became head of the Manchester director-area. He was appointed managing director in 1944 and later in the year, deputy chairman. On his retirement from executive duties in 1952, he was appointed chairman of the board.

He was joint treasurer of the National Amalgamated Approved Society from 1944 to 1946, and treasurer from 1946 until the approved societies were taken over by the Ministry of National Insurance in 1948. He has been a member of the executive of the Industrial Life Offices Association since 1945. He is married, with a son and a daughter.

In the First World War he enlisted in the Artists Rifles in 1915, and was later commissioned to the Manchester Regiment. Severely wounded in 1917 he was discharged in December, 1918, with the rank of Lieutenant. In the Second War, he served in the Special Constabulary.

He was a Sale Urban District Councillor from 1927 to 1938, and for several years a governor of two schools in Sale. He was at one time a member of the management committee of the Altrincham General Hospital, and has been a Justice of the Peace for the County of Chester since 1933. He has been president for many years of the Sale Golf and Cricket Clubs, and a vice-president of the Lancashire County Cricket Club.

He has always been interested in birds and animals, and has been very successful in competitions and on the Show bench. In 1958 he won the Waterloo Cup. Other interests are reading and gardening.

JAMES PROCTOR-PEARSON, J.P., is a great-grandson of the Founder. Educated privately, he joined the company in 1925, and spent several years in the actuarial department before being transferred in 1929 to the investment department, where his principal interest became the house purchase section. In 1932 he was elected a director, and served as joint house purchase manager from 1946 to 1951, when he was appointed deputy chairman of the board.

In the Second War, he served in the Royal Observer Corps from 1938 to 1942, then transferring to the Air Transport Auxiliary, in which he remained until the end of hostilities. He is married, with a son and two daughters.

For many years he has taken an active part in public affairs. He was a member of the Manchester City Council from 1938 to 1946, and in 1949 was appointed a Justice of the Peace for the City of Manchester.

He is interested in golf, gardening and, particularly, photography.

MAURICE WILCOCK HOLGATE, M.A., is a son of J. Wilcock Holgate, the late president of the company. He was educated at the Leys School and Christ's College, Cambridge where he took his Law Tripos. He became a barrister-at-law in 1934, and practised in London. He joined the company in 1946 as joint secretary, and was elected a director in 1947, becoming managing director in 1952. The same year he was appointed to the executive of the Industrial Life Offices Association, becoming vice-chairman in 1955 and chairman from 1956 to 1958. He served on the legal committee of the association from 1947 to 1956, and has been a member of the Industrial Assurance Council since 1952. He is married, with one daughter.

During the War he served for six years in the Royal Navy,

mainly in destroyers. He was mentioned in dispatches, and demobilised in December, 1945, as a Lieutenant-Commander.

Interested in out-of-doors pursuits, he spends much of his spare time in gardening, fishing and beagling.

FRANCIS HARRY THORNTON is a grandson of Henry Thornton, the pioneer for the company in the Warrington area. Educated at Grove Park School, Wrexham, he joined the company in 1914, at the Warrington office, the headquarters of the director-area controlled by his father, Wm. Eber Thornton. He passed through each department in the divisional office, and was later transferred to field work as a travelling inspector, becoming joint divisional manager for the area in 1919. He was elected to the board in 1939, and retired from executive duties in 1940.

In the First World War he enlisted in the Royal Engineers (Signals), and was demobilised in 1918 with the rank of Sergeant. He is married, with two daughters.

He has been a keen motorist for many years, and is interested in cine-photography and also astronomy, of which he writes in a technical periodical which he has edited for a number of years.

RICHARD CARR GREEN is a great-grandson of the Founder and the son of J. Proctor Green, formerly deputy chairman of the company. Educated at Stanmore Park Preparatory School, and Harrow, he joined the staff in November, 1929. He began at once in the investment department, and this aspect of the business has been his concern ever since. He was elected to the board in 1944. In 1946 he was appointed joint house purchase manager, and in 1952 was made investment secretary in Manchester jointly with R. F. Pennington in London.

Prior to the Second War, he was a Territorial and was called up in August, 1939. He served in the Lancashire Fusiliers from Private to

Lieutenant, and was demobilised in 1945. He is married, with one son.

He is a trustee of the Manchester and Salford Trustee Savings Bank, and a member of the finance sub-committee of the Manchester University. He is chairman of the local branch of the Conservative Association.

A keen gardener and fisherman, he is also interested in agriculture.

SAMUEL GEORGE LEIGH, F.I.A., joined the company at the age of 13. Educated locally, shortly after leaving school he began to study for the actuarial examinations. He gained his Fellowship of the Institute in 1912, by which time he was principal actuarial clerk under W. H. Aldcroft. He was promoted to be assistant actuary in 1914, deputy actuary in 1926, and general manager in 1930. He was appointed a director in 1944, and retired from executive duties in 1946. He has now served the company for over 62 years, for a longer period than any other individual in the company's history. For several years he was a member of the actuarial committee of the Industrial Life Offices Association, and was one of a number of actuaries who advised the association during discussions preliminary to the passing of the Industrial Assurance Act, 1923. He gave evidence before the Cohen Committee prior to its report in 1933: and was at one time tutor in mathematics and actuarial science at the Manchester School of Commerce. He is a widower, with one daughter, and his interests to-day are reading, photography, and the playing of bowls.

He is the author of *A Guide to Life Assurance*, for many years a text-book on the subject.

JAMES ARTHUR BOOTH is a grandson of Robert Moss, who followed the first secretary, George Robins, and served in that capacity for nearly forty years. Educated at Glossop Grammar School, he joined the company in 1914 at the age of 16. His early business years were spent in the actuarial department, the then usual training ground for new members of the staff. In 1920 he was transferred to the secretary's department, under his uncle, John W. Moss: and on the death of the latter in 1946, he was appointed joint secretary. He was elected to the board in 1947, and retired in July, 1958, after 44 years service, retaining his position as director.

In 1917, at the age of 18, he became a Rifleman in the Queen's Westminster Rifles, in which he served until wounded and discharged in 1918. He is married, with two sons.

In his younger days he was a well-known figure in Derbyshire League cricket. His interests now are golf and gardening.

CYRIL CLEGG, F.I.A., is a grandson of John Moon, a prominent fieldman with the Prudential Assurance Co., Ltd., who held an agency in 1852 with the British Industry, the first industrial assurance company. Educated at the Manchester Grammar School, he joined the company in 1909 at the age of 16, and at once began his actuarial studies. Qualifying as Fellow in 1920, he was appointed assistant actuary in 1926, actuary in 1930, joint general manager in 1946, and on his retirement in 1953, a director of the company.

In his early days, encouraged by W. H. Aldcroft, he took part in Chartered Insurance Institute affairs, and was president of the Manchester Insurance Institute from 1931 to 1932. He was a pioneer of the inclusion of industrial assurance in the institute syllabus, and served on the examiners committee from 1930 to 1945 He was a member of the actuarial committee of the Industrial Life Offices Association from 1930 to 1946, and of the standing committee from 1948 to 1953. He served on two of the sub-committees set up by the association to consider evidence given before the Cohen Committee. He was the founder and first president of the Manchester Actuarial Society, 1929 to 1931, and at one time a tutor in actuarial subjects at the Manchester School of Commerce. He is married, with three sons.

In the First World War he served in the Royal Garrison Artillery from 1915 to 1919, being mentioned in dispatches and demobilised in 1919 with the rank of Lieutenant.

He is a governor of the Manchester High School for Girls, and has been honorary treasurer since 1940.

He has represented Lancashire, and later Cheshire, at lawn tennis: and now living in the Lake District, is interested in nature and in reading.

Appendix B

Office-bearers: Past and Present

PRESIDENT:

J. WILCOCK HOLGATE	1952–1955

CHAIRMEN:

WILLIAM PROCTOR	1884–1898
JAMES WILCOCK, J.P. . . .	1898–1911
R. W. GREEN, J.P. . . .	1912–1922
JAS. S. PROCTOR	1922–1928
J. WILCOCK HOLGATE	1928–1952
WM. PROCTOR SMITH, J.P. . . .	1952–

DEPUTY CHAIRMEN:

J. WILCOCK HOLGATE	1926–1928
J. PROCTOR GREEN, J.P.	1928–1944
WM. PROCTOR SMITH, J.P. . . .	1944–1950
WM. PROCTOR SMITH, J.P. ⎫ J. PROCTOR-PEARSON, J.P. ⎬ . .	1951–1952
J. PROCTOR-PEARSON, J.P. . . .	1952–

MANAGING DIRECTORS:

JAMES PROCTOR	1872–1888
PHILIP SMITH ⎫ JAS. S. PROCTOR ⎬	1914–1925
JAS. S. PROCTOR ⎫ J. PROCTOR GREEN, J.P. ⎬ . .	1925–1928
J. PROCTOR GREEN, J.P. . . .	1928–1944
WM. PROCTOR SMITH, J.P. . . .	1944–1951
M. WILCOCK HOLGATE, M.A. . .	1951–

149

GENERAL MANAGERS:

WM. BRADBURN	1858–1865 (presumably)
GEORGE BRIDGE	1865–1870 (approx.)
JAMES PROCTOR	1870 (approx.)–1888
WM. PROCTOR	1888–1898
JAMES PROCTOR (JNR.) R. W. GREEN, J.P.	1898–1902
R. W. GREEN, J.P. JOHN W. PROCTOR	1902–1909
R. W. GREEN, J.P. PHILIP SMITH	1909–1912
PHILIP SMITH JAS. S. PROCTOR	1912–1914
J. PROCTOR GREEN, J.P. W. H. ALDCROFT, F.I.A.	1914–1925
W. H. ALDCROFT, F.I.A.	1925–1930
S. G. LEIGH, F.I.A.	1930–1946
CYRIL CLEGG, F.I.A. L. ASHMORE, M. COMM.	1946–1948
CYRIL CLEGG, F.I.A. E. G. ALMOND	1948–1953
E. G. ALMOND	1953–1955
H. S. SEVER, F.I.A. BARRY F. HICKS, F.F.A.	1955–

SECRETARIES:

GEORGE ROBINS	1858–1871
HENRY BRIDGE	1872 (approx.)–1884
ROBERT MOSS, J.P.	1884–1923
JOHN W. MOSS	1923–1946

SECRETARIES CONTD.:

M. WILCOCK HOLGATE, M.A. }
JAMES A. BOOTH }   .   .   1946–1958

M. WILCOCK HOLGATE, M.A. }
PETER M. WILLIAMS }   .   .   1958–

ACTUARIES:

(Consulting) THOS. JOSH. C. L. BORDMAN, LL.D., F.S.S.   .   1871–1891
(Consulting) JAMES CHATHAM, F.I.A.   .   .   .   1891
          W. H. ALDCROFT, F.I.A.   .   .   .   1896–1930
          CYRIL CLEGG, F.I.A.   .   .   .   1930–1946
          BARRY F. HICKS, F.F.A.   .   .   .   1946–1955
          N. W. ROSS, F.I.A.   .   .   .   1955–

AGENCY MANAGER:

ALBERT SWIFT   1930–1937

GENERAL INSPECTORS:

J. G. MARRIOTT   .   .   .   1913–1923
WM. EDWARDS, M.B.E.   .   .   1919–1925
T. R. MITCHELL   .   .   .   1919–1923
JABEZ PEARSON   .   .   .   1919–1923
ALBERT SWIFT   .   .   .   1919–1930
J. I. NATHAN   .   .   .   1934–1947
J. T. BOOTHMAN   .   .   .   1934–1947
C. B. ADAMS   .   .   .   1944–1949
G. A. FILER   .   .   .   1947–1952
*H. E. BARBER   .   .   .   1949–1958
*A. M. MORGAN   .   .   .   1949–
*G. PARKIN   .   .   .   1952–1958

* Styled " Area Managers "

Appendix C

Comparative Statistics

INDUSTRIAL BRANCH

Year	Premiums	Percentage, commission and expenses to premiums	Net new sums assured	Net assurances in force	Fund
	£		£	£	£
1888	483,405	52.07			213,601
1898	930,999	52.86			495,487
1908	1,702,696	48.76		30,135,002	1,619,207
1918	2,658,607	42.50	7,399,979	48,241,047	3,737,034
1928	4,632,776	37.26	16,952,369	82,568,393	13,222,558
1938	5,994,706	32.83	15,861,062	115,604,548	27,808,404
1948	8,324,809	26.83	11,833,403	157,867,029	50,105,808
1956	10,327,594	28.37	17,316,943	199,830,163	64,556,043

ORDINARY BRANCH

Year	Premiums	Percentage, commission and expenses to premiums	Net new sums assured	Net assurances in force	Fund
	£		£	£	£
1888	13,794	10.00			18,831
1898	257,885	9.94	1,255,725		795,719
1908	764,441	9.95	2,029,498	14,336,058	4,261,088
1918	1,563,322	10.00	3,663,588	28,325,412	11,360,223
1928	3,702,345	16.14	6,377,442	60,501,567	27,677,034
1938	4,691,372	14.03	7,894,878	84,479,000	38,688,366
1948	6,367,145	13.38	13,583,699	114,589,451	49,571,032
1956	7,997,997	13.12	16,798,818	158,361,396	68,480,430

How the Company Celebrated

ANY centenary, naturally, is an event; and in the case of the Refuge, with its strong family spirit, it was felt that it should be celebrated, not only with pride in achievement, but also with some form of festivity on the lines of the old English " cakes and ale ". Having in mind the large number of people involved, it was obviously impossible to invite everybody to a giant party, and so the affair was dealt with in stages.

The first people to be considered were the pensioners, for whom it was happily found possible either to make annual payments additional to their pensions, or to make cash gifts—dependent in each case on the date of retirement. The present staff, both at chief office and in the field, were not forgotten, and gifts of cash sums were made varying with the length of service.

Since the company had been so closely connected with the City of Manchester for so many years, it was earnestly desired to make some sort of gift to the Corporation to mark the occasion, and the idea happily emerged of offering a travelling mace to complement the existing massive and heavy symbol of office which successive Lord Mayors had hitherto been required to convey with them on their official visits. To the great pleasure of the Board the offer was accepted; and at an informal ceremony in the Town Hall the new mace was formally handed over by the chairman of the company, Wm. Proctor Smith, J.P., to the Lord Mayor, Alderman James E. Fitzsimons, J.P. Photographs of the event, and of the symbol, are shown herein, and the following is a description of this addition to the insignia of the City's leading citizen: It is made of silver, is 35 inches long, and weighs 54 ounces as compared with the present mace, which weighs 15 lb. The head bears the arms of the

City, enamelled and richly gilt.   The four branches which protect the Arms are surmounted by a circlet of cross patée and fleur-de-lys, above which are displayed the Royal Arms in gold on a red enamelled background.   Below the head, in rose leaf decoration, are the badge of the City and the Arms of the Company.   The whole is made in two sections, for transport in a specially designed case made of hide, bearing a silver plate engraved with the City Arms.

Finally it was decided to hold a series of Occasions, to one or other of which each member of the staff would be invited.   The week June 9th—13th was chosen for the entertainment in stages of the staff of chief office and the senior members of the field staff, whilst the remaining members of the field staff would later in the year be the company's guests at a series of luncheons to be held in thirteen centres covering the whole of the country.

For some period before and after the centenary week, chief office was made to look very gay, with flags flying, ornamental shields on each of the three buildings, and principally—and most happily—with each of the three entrances banked with flowers, shrubs and ornamental trees.

The effect was rather surprising.   It had not been thought that the display would create so much interest amongst the passers-by, and it was an unexpected pleasure to receive letters such as the following:

"As one of the teeming thousands who work in Oxford Street, I would like to congratulate your Company on attaining its Centenary . . . But what has given me, a mere passer-by, such unbounded pleasure is the gaiety of your building, . . . It is a truly magnificent show . . . As I pass each day I am lifted out of the drab streets of Manchester and go my way with a lighter step and a gladder heart."

The opening dinner on the Monday for the management, senior members of the chief office staff, and retired departmental heads was a great success, and set the note for all the remaining events of the week. The fact was that all the guests there, and especially the pensioners, were enormously proud of the company—and therefore of themselves. The general impression can best be conveyed by remarks from two different speakers: From the company side " The toast is not, as usual, ' To the Staff ', but ' To our honoured and sincere friends ' ", and from a staff speaker " Thank you for a gracious evening—a perfect gift from our hosts ".

Perhaps the highlight of the entire week was the thanksgiving service in the old City Church of St. Ann on the Tuesday morning. For this the company was indebted to the kindness of the Rector, the Rev. Canon. Eric Saxon, B.A., B.D., who personally approached the office, and for so important an event in the company's history offered the Board the freedom of his church throughout the week. The company had hesitated to ask for facilities for a service, for such a thanksgiving must not bear any suggestion of advertisement or self-glory, and the Board was deeply grateful for the opportunity thus generously afforded them of giving thanks for many mercies extended to the Refuge over so many years. The service will long be remembered by those whom it was possible to compress into the ancient church—built in 1712 in green fields, and ever since then a centre and focus of religious life for Manchester citizens, not only on Sundays but on every working day of the year.

The luncheon the same day to the management and senior members of the field staff afforded another opportunity for the display of senti-ments of pride and loyalty amongst men who, unlike those at chief office with its closely-knit association, could be excused for regarding the company, as it were, from afar, almost as an impersonal thing. Far from it; the atmosphere was again one of affection, and perhaps it was explained in a remark made by an old member of the staff in replying to the toast to the guests—a former inspector, retired for 23 years, aged 83, who said, " Looking back on my life I know I could not have chosen a more sympathetic employer, nor could I have had a happier business career."

The banquet on the Thursday to all the company's friends within the business of insurance and to its connections with other allied activities was a most memorable occasion. It was held—to the surprise of many guests—actually in chief office, which only the previous day had been in full operation in the ordinary fashion. By the evening of the following day it had been transformed, by devoted work which went on all through the night and day, with carpets, flowers, shrubs, and even—in the dining hall—a waterfall complete with pool and goldfish. The whole effect was quite striking and gave obvious pleasure, not only to the organisers—who naturally *would* like it—but also to the guests who were under no such compulsion. The success of the evening was encouraged by three novel ideas:—There was a very small top table, all the others being so arranged around the hall as to ensure that no one had his or her back to the speakers: to each table were appointed a host and hostess to whom were attached one or two members of the staff to act as marshals, whose duty it was to collect each of the guests of their table as they were announced, and to deliver them to their host and hostess, who would then keep them together so that all would know one another before descending to the hall: and finally, the idea was adopted of having the speeches—few in number—during the meal rather than afterwards. Opportunity and time were thus afforded the various Tables to break up and the guests to mingle and converse with their various friends.

In replying to the toast to the City, the Lord Mayor referred to what he called the gracious act of the Refuge in presenting the corporation with its new mace, and said he was happy to be associated with a company with such a record of service. It is worth recording a remark of the proposer of the toast, who pointed out a likeness between the Rolls-Royce car and the Refuge: both highly successful, and both begun by being put together in a back street in Manchester.

The following day, Friday, was the day for all those members of chief office who could not be accommodated at the dinner earlier in the week, including the restaurant staff and the cleaners. Predominantly youthful as they were, the occasion clearly called for a light touch and the party spirit, the outcome being two special trains—with decorated engines—which conveyed all the guests to Blackpool, with lunch (with no speeches), the freedom of the Tower and Winter Gardens, a late meal, and a return by special trains, with chartered buses waiting at the stations to take the revellers home. The combination of perfect weather and infectious high spirits made the event a tremendous success—what a happy note on which to finish up the centenary week !

Finally, a special trip was arranged for the maintenance staff who could not be spared during the week itself. The party, exclusively male, numbered 34, and the members travelled by train to Liverpool and thence by boat to Llandudno, lunch and an evening meal being served on board. This party was adult in character, but credible reports make it abundantly clear that high spirits are not the prerogative of the young. Once again the weather was ideal: a fitting conclusion to the Celebrations and a cheerful opening to the Company's second century.

xix

3rd June, 1958
Presentation of Mace

9th June, 1958
Dinner to the
Management
and Senior
Members of
Chief Office
Staff

xxi

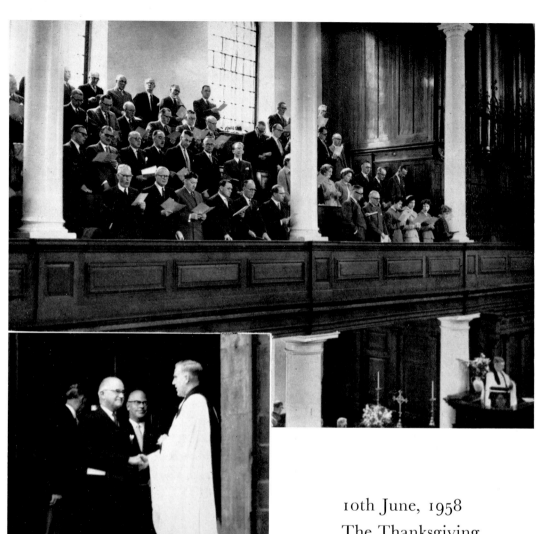

10th June, 1958
The Thanksgiving
Service

10th June, 1958
Luncheon to
the Manage-
ment and Senior
Members of the
Field Staff

12th June, 1958
Reception at
Chief Office

12th June, 1958
Dinner at Chief Office
The Chairman's table

M. Wilcock
Holgate's
Table

J. A. Booth's
Table

Cyril Clegg's
Table

13th June, 1958
Visit to Blackpool

Luncheon, Blackpool

xxviii

Blackpool

18th June, 1958
Visit to Llandudno

xxx

INDEX

ACTS OF PARLIAMENT

—Assurance Companies, 1909   75

—Courts (Emergency Powers), 1914 ... ... 86, 100

—Industrial Assurance, 1923 ...   99

—Industrial Assurance and Friendly Societies, 1948 ... 125

—Industrial Assurance and Friendly Societies, 1948 (Amendment), 1958 ... 125

—Industrial Assurance and Friendly Societies (Emergency Protection from Forfeiture), 1948 117

—Joint Stock Companies, 1862   24-29

—Life Assurance Companies, 1870 ... ... 43, 46

—National Health Insurance, 1911 76

—National Insurance, 1946 ... 125

accountants, Refuge 80

actuary (Bordman) 44

actuary, first qualified 65

actuaries, list of 151

actuary's reports 44, 47, 66

Adams, Henry 25, 26, 48, 138

Adams, Wm. 56, 138

advertising department 133

agency manager 151

agency staff, size of 89, 119

agents, occupations of first ... 17

agents' remuneration ... 18, 84

agreements with other offices   60, 61

air raid shelter collections ... 120

air raid shelters, chief office ... 121

Albert, The 42

Aldcroft, W. H. 65, 66, 74, 76, 78, 94, 109, 122, 123

Almond, E. G. 126

Ancient Order of Foresters ... 54

" Anglo-Bengalee Disinterested Loan and Life Assurance " 42

annual reports 35

approved societies 76, 77, 79

approved societies, dissolution of 125

approved societies, valuation of 79

arms, grant of 128

arrears 102, 106, 110

articles of association 29

Ashmore, Lawrence 96

Aspinall, Ven. Noel Lake ... 104

assets 45

Association of Industrial Assurance Companies and Collecting Friendly Societies (see
also Industrial Life Offices
Association) 62, 69, 99

auditors 80

automatic free policies 100

BAY HORSE INN 53

bee-hive sign 82, 128

beginning of Refuge 6, 12

Beveridge committee 124

Beveridge report and industrial
assurance 124

Birkett, Stanley 112

Birchall, Miss 73

blocking of debits 91, 92

bomb damaged offices 120

bond form, agents' 57

bonuses ... 66, 108, 109, 111, 118

bonus, early collectors' ... 18, 26

bonus, first O.B. 66

first I.B. 109

bonuses reduced in war 118

Booth, James A. 146

Bordman, Thos. Josh. C. L. 44,
52, 66

Bradburn, Wm. ... 9, 12, 13, 14,
18, 23, 24, 30, 31, 32, 33, 34, 37, 41, 53

Bridge, George 23, 30, 33, 34,
37, 38, 41, 48, 136, 137

Bridge, Henry 48, 56, 137

British Industries in 20th
Century ... ... xi, 5

British Industry, The ... 63, 147

burial clubs 2, 3, 4, 5, 8

burial, Roman 1

Byng, Hon. John 3

CAPITAL 29, 57, 135

cash book, first 6, 7, 12, 13, 16

celebration of centenary 156

Centenary Celebrations

—banquet ... 158, xxiv, xxv, xxvi

—cash grants 156

—presentation mace ... 156, xx

—staff dinner ... ... 157, xxi

—staff luncheon ... ... 158, xxiii

—staff outings ... 159, 160, xxvii,
xxviii, xxix, xxx

—thanksgiving service ... 158, xxii

certificate of insurance, early 14

chairman, first 56

chairmen, list of 149

change of name ... 14, 27, 54

Chatham, James 66

children's assurances ... 76, 100

civic week, Manchester, 1926 ... 107

claim ratios 88

claims, first 13

claims payments 23, 45

Clegg, Cyril 107, 109, 111, 126, 147

clerks, recruitment of 73

coal lock out 66

coal strike 84, 106

Cohen Committee 81, 111

collections in air raid shelters 120

collectors, early 17

Collegia, Roman 1

committee of management, first 8

company, formation of 24, 27, 29

conference hall 113

cotton strike 66

Crescent Inn Money Society ... 14

DARNTON, MR. 24

death benefit, national insurance 125

debits, increase in size 92

deposit with High Court ... 100

depression, ... 102, 106, 110

deputy chairmen, list of ... 149

diamond jubilee of Refuge ... 104

Dickens, Charles 42

directors' fees 30

directors' qualifications 29

directors' report, 1866 35

District Bank 30

districts, number of ... 85, 89

duplication of records 121

Dukinfield (see offices—Astley
street)

EARLY CLAIMS 13

Edwards, Wm. 78, 93

emergency generator 122

engineer, resident 113

European, The 20, 42

expenses (and expense ratio) 23,
26, 40, 57, 85, 88,
91, 100, 110, 111, 112

FEDERATED EMPLOYERS' INSUR-
ANCE ASSOCIATION ... 95, 131, 132

Ferrand, J. H. 23, 35, 41, 48

finance committee 41

first actuary 63, 65

Fitzsimons, Ald. J. E. 156

Fletcher, Thomas 8

Foley, P. J. 62

"Founder, The"—see James
Proctor

France, Joshua 9

free policies 100

Free Trade Hall luncheon ... 104

funds, life 46, 47

funeral expense policies ... 75, 76

GENERAL BRANCH, ESTABLISH-
MENT OF 94, 95, 131

general inspectors 84, 151

general managers, list of 150

general strike 106

George, David Lloyd ... 76, 83

gilds 2

Gladstone, W. E. 27

gold standard 110

goodwill campaign 127

Government inquiries ... 27, 98, 111, 124

Government loans, support for 88, 118

gratuities on death, staff ... 98

Green, J. Proctor 70, 78, 99, 105, 122

Green, Richard C. 145

Green, R. W. 70, 78, 80, 103, 122

Green, Wm. P. 80

Guide to Life Assurance, A ... 146

Guild of Insurance Officials ... 95

" HAREM ", THE 72

Hargreaves, C. J. 113

Harrison, Cyril C. 81

Harrison, John 80, 111

Hart Street, Manchester ... 13

Haselden, John 8, 13

health insurance, national 76, 77, 78, 79

History of Life Assurance xi, xii, 1

History of Industrial Life Assurance 111

Holgate, J. Wilcock ... 70, 78, 94 108, 127, 129

Holgate, M. Wilcock ... 70, 74, 126, 127, 144

Holmes, Miss 121

Home Service Insurance ... ix

house purchase 107

INDUSTRIAL ASSURANCE COMMISSIONER 100, 116

Industrial Assurance Council 127, 130, 144

Industrial and Life Assurance Amalgamation Company Ltd. Dublin 115

industrial branch (see chap. VI)

industrial branch bonus ... 108, 109

industrial branch funds, ... 45, 46, 47

industrial branch valuations ... 100

industrial depression 102, 106, 110

Industrial Life Offices Association ... 70, 81, 103, 105, 108, 122, 124, 130, 143, 144, 146

influenza epidemics ... 66, 69, 88

insurable interest 125

investment office, London ... 132

Irish (Eire) business 115

Jack, Prof. Fingland 1, 4

Jarvis, G. A. 99

Jones, Edgar 96, 99

Jones, John 8

LABOUR'S NATIONALISATION PROPOSALS 126

lady clerks, first 72

INDEX

Leader, Selina 17, 85

Leigh, S. G. 25, 99, 109,
                                    111, 146

Letter from Past for Present ...   48

life-of-another policies   125

Livesey Street office, Manchester
                                    16, 48, 93

Liverpool Victoria   54

Liverpool Victoria, agreement
    with   60

livery companies   2

loan branch   35

loans to Refuge   14

London office, first   33

Lord Mayor of Manchester ...   156

MACCLESFIELD, WORKING MAN'S
    BENEFIT SOCIETY   14

mace presented to Manchester
                                    156, xx

managing directors, list of   ...   149

Manchester Actuarial Society ...   147

Manchester Arms Hotel ...   15, 53

Manchester Insurance Institute   147

Manchester and Liverpool Dis-
    trict Bank   30

Manchester and Salford Burial
    Society, take over of   15

Manchester and Salford relief
    fund (S.A. war)   69

Manchester Unity of Oddfel-
    lows   54

Manchester civic week   107

Manchester Regiment   87

Manchester Ship Canal   55

Marriott, J. G.   84

Martin Chuzzlewit   42

mechanisation, chief office   26, 58,
                                    92, 133

medical examination   21

millionth O.B. policy   105

minimum wage demand   ...   84

Ministry of National Insurance
                                    77, 125

Mitchell, T. R.   93

Moon, John   147

Morrah, Dermot   111

Moss, John W.   138

Moss, Robert   ...   25, 38, 56, 58, 137

Mottershead, F. W. D.   78

NAME, CHANGE OF   14

National Amalgamated Ap-
    proved Society 77, 78, 79,
        94, 103, 105, 108, 122, 130, 143

National Conference of Indus-
    trial Assurance Approved
    Societies   130

national health insurance   ...   76,
                                    77, 78, 79

National Insurance, Ministry of
                                    77, 125

national savings collectors   ...   125

nationalisation, opposition to   126

new business in war   118

O.B. MILLIONTH POLICY ... 105

—millionth premium £ 105

Offices, Chief

—Albert Street, Manchester ... 39

—Astley Street, Dukinfield ... 13, 15, 18, 39

—Blackfriars, Manchester ... 39

—Corporation Street, Manchester, 11-13 ... ... 39, 53

—Corporation Street, Manchester, 85-89 52

—Halliwell Lane, Manchester 63

—Hart Street, Manchester 13, 64

—Peter Street, Manchester ... 63

—Oxford Street, Manchester 53, 63, 64, 81, 112, 131

officers, first 8

Onslow, Lord 98

ordinary branch expansion ... 46

ordinary branch funds ... 46, 47

ordinary branch, separation of I.B. from 46

PARMINTER (ASSISTANT) 121

Parmoor committee 98

Parnell, W. J. 121

"part surrenders" 110

Paton-Williams, Rev. Canon F. 131

pauper's grave 3

Pearl, agreement with 61

Pearson, Jabez 93, 94

pension schemes, staff ... 98, 114

"permitted" relatives 76, 100, 125

Pim Hole Club 34, 48

Plummer, Dr. Alfred ... ... xi, 5

poaching of members ... 59, 60

policies in war, maintenance of 116

Poor Law, Tudor 2

Post Office insurance scheme 27, 125

Pratt, Henry 14

Pratt, John Tidd 7, 31, 44

premiums, growth of 112

premium income 23, 45, 55

premium receipt books 62

premiums, unpaid in war ... 87

president 11, 129, 149

printing department 113

Proctor, James ... 9, 10, 12, 16, 23, 30, 33, 34, 35, 36, 37, 41, 48, 58, 62, 114, 122, 136

Proctor (Junr.), James 56

Proctor, James S. 70, 78, 103, 104, 108, 122, 136

Proctor, John W. 70, 80

Proctor, William 41, 48, 58, 64, 67

Proctor-Pearson, J. 144

progress in early years ... 15, 20

protection of I.B. policies in war 86, 117

Prudential, The ... 99, 127, 147

publicity, Refuge 133

QUIET GILL MONEY SOCIETY ... 14

INDEX

REASSURANCE 20

records duplicated 121

recruitment of staff ... 73, 74

Refuge growth (statistics) ... 152

Refuge Assurance Company Ltd. 54

Refuge Field Staff Association 96, 97, 99

Refuge Friend in Deed

—formation of 6

—passing of 28, 31, 35, 44

Refuge Friend in Deed Life Assurance and Sick Fund Friendly Society ... 14, 29

Refuge Friendly Society ... 14

Refuge Friendly Society Ltd. 27, 29

Refuge Life and Sick Friendly Society 14, 30

Refuge Staff Council ... 95, 99

Refugium Rebus Adversis ... 129

Registrar of Friendly Societies 6, 7, 52

Remuneration

—agents' 18, 26, 57, 84

—directors' 40, 57

—first officers' 18

—staff, chief office 96

rent, first 13

report, 1866, annual 35

reversionary bonus (see bonus)

Robins, George 9, 10, 13, 18, 23, 24, 30, 36, 38, 47, 56, 137

Robins, Joe 8, 10, 48

Rochefoucald, François de ... 3

Roman collegia 1, 4

Royal Liver 54

rules 7, 13, 21

SAXON, REV. CANON ERIC 158

secretary, first 10

secretaries, list of 150

separation of I.B. and O.B. ... 46

share capital 29, 57, 135

shares, original 6, 12

Sheffield district 25

Shutt, Thos. 56, 140

sick club levy 4

sick fund created 7

sickness insurance experience 21, 22, 32, 37, 45, 46

Sinclair, Thomas 9

Sixtieth anniversary celebrations as Limited Company ... 104

Slack, John 9

Smith, Philip 70, 78, 105

Smith, Wm. Proctor ... 70, 78, 129, 131, 143, 156

Solicitors, Company's

—Darnton, Mr. 24

—Green, Wm. P. 80

—Harrison, Cyril C. 81

—Harrison, John 80

—Proctor, John W. 80

South African War 67, 68, 69

INDEX

staff council 95, 99
—dining hall 113
—gratuities on death 98
—problems in war 85, 119
—recruitment of 73, 74
—relations 95, 96
—remuneration and pensions 95, 98, 114
—size of 89, 119
statistics (growth of company) 152
Stock Exchange quotation ... 134
*Survey of Economic Develop-
ment* xi
Sutcliffe, Joseph 16
Swift, Albert 93, 94, 109

TABLEAUX, REFUGE 107
tables, benefit 52
take-over of societies ... 14, 15
telephone, first 58
thanksgiving service 153
Thornton, Francis H. 145
Thornton, Henry ... 24, 26, 48, 139
tower, the Refuge 82
trade clubs 4
trade union, Refuge 97
transferring 59, 60
treasurer, first 10
treasurer's book ... 6, 7, 12, 13, 16
treating of agents 53

UNPAID PREMIUMS IN WAR ... 87

VALUATIONS 47, 66, 100, 110, 111
valuation of approved societies 79
volunteers for Great War ... 87
volunteers for S.A. war 69

WALTON, WATTS AND CO. 80
War
—new business during 118
—grants to service men 68, 87, 119
—staff problems in 119
—casualties, staff ... 69, 88, 130
—claims 68, 88, 117
—clause, suspension of 86
—contact with policyholders 119
—grants to staff in 87, 88
—memorials ... 82, 103, 108, 130
Ward, Thomas 8, 12
Warrington district 24
Wars
—South African 67, 68, 69
—Great War 84
—Second Great War 116
Waterhouse, Alfred 64
Waterhouse, Paul 81
Whitaker, J. B. 114
Wilcock, James 42, 56, 67, 80, 140
Winfrey, William 16
women, employment of ... 86, 87, 89, 92
Woodcock, James 9, 10, 35, 37, 56
Working Man's Benefit Society, Macclesfield 14
ZETA 82